Like Thunder

—

POETS RESPOND TO

VIOLENCE IN AMERICA

EDITED BY VIRGIL SUÁREZ

AND RYAN G. VAN CLEAVE

Like Thunder

Ψ

UNIVERSITY OF IOWA PRESS

Iowa City

University of Iowa Press,
Iowa City 52242
Copyright © 2002 by
Virgil Suárez and Ryan G. Van Cleave
All rights reserved
Printed in the United States of America
Design by Richard Hendel
http://www.uiowa.edu/~uipress

The publication of this book was
generously supported by the University
of Iowa Foundation.

Printed on acid-free paper

02 03 04 05 06 C 5 4 3 2 1
02 03 04 05 06 P 5 4 3 2 1

Library of Congress
Cataloging-in-Publication Data

Like thunder: poets respond to violence
in America / edited by Virgil Suárez and
Ryan G. Van Cleave.
p.   cm.
Includes index.
ISBN 0-87745-791-3 (cloth),
ISBN 0-87745-792-1 (pbk.)
    1. American poetry—20th century.
2. Violence—Poetry.   I. Suárez,
Virgil, 1962–   II. Van Cleave,
Ryan G., 1972–

PS595.V55 L55   2002
811'.54080355—dc21   2001052280

CONTENTS

The idea for this anthology began during the school year of 1999–2000 with the two of us lunching twice a week at our favorite Tallahassee restaurants, and even there, immersed in all the Diet Cokes, *cafecitos*, Cuban sandwiches, french fries, and BBQ chicken we could eat, somehow the discussion always revolved around the horrors of the world. Columbine. Waco. The Atlanta child murders. Jeffrey Dahmer. Oklahoma City. The FSU student shot execution-style over spring break 2000 and left in an abandoned dorm room, unnoticed for a week. Even our students were obsessing on violence and how it's permeated into the psyche of America; they wrote about it in their composition essays, in their poems, in their short stories, and in their journals. So it's no real surprise that after we were at the tail-end of *American Diaspora: Poetry of Displacement* — in need of a new project to direct our energies — the idea of an anthology on violence in America immediately reared its ugly head. So we decided to edit this anthology, us, David, to this massive social problem, Goliath. But that's what it's all about, we knew — standing up and letting your voice be heard.

Violence. It's in the newspapers. It's on TV. It's in our movies, our jokes, our children's toys. If we've learned anything during our lives here in America, it's this: no one is safe. By that we mean that violence appears not just in the projects or on foreign soil, but in the unlikeliest of places. In a church. In a post office. In a McDonald's. And we need to understand it, to some degree, so we can make peace with it. Accept it. And then live our lives despite it. That's what these writers do in wonderful and engaging poetry — they reflect and meditate, rage and bless as they confront the evergrowing issue of violence in America, and ultimately, we think, offer us what we desperately need: hope. There is a tomorrow, there is a future. Through poetry, we learn what it is to be human and fragile, but sometimes wonderfully so.

Much of the early discussion about this book stemmed from a desire to organize it in some meaningful way, break it down into components, themes, or units we might more easily understand and compartmentalize. But the more we examined the individual poems, the more we realized they were reflective of the violence around us: the themes were varied, the styles clashing, the voices calm and yet frantic. To select groups of poems and label them "School Murders" or "Domestic Violence" doesn't do these poems justice. Each is a fully realized, complex meditation on the issues and ramifications of violence in our society, both the micro and the macro. They defy easy classification and simple analysis, and that's why we knew this anthology was so necessary.

When we were young, we worried about the Red Menace or being blown to smithereens by atomic weapons. Nowadays, what American children worry about is being in the wrong place at the wrong time when a drug deal goes bad. Or that some kid with an Uzi in his locker has a rotten day. Or that some irate government employees decide that it's *this* city block they'll blast with a truck bomb just to make a point. With that type of fear looming larger than the back-of-the-mind worries of Mother Russia or Fidel Castro or Middle Eastern terrorists, now more than ever we need an antidote, a cure, a way to navigate through these everpresent concerns. What we offer here is poetry, which, as Michael Klein recently wrote, "is the best truth in a time when there isn't very much truth."

From the domestic violence in Kim Addonizio's "From Then to Now" and John Lundberg's "Chivalry," to the meditations on violence in Gaylord Brewer's "Essays on Excess and Escape" and Brigitte Byrd's "Top Stories," to the media-covered horrors of Michael Bugeja's "Littleton" and Jeffrey Clapp's "Kaczynski" and Richard Newman's "Salem, Indiana, 1983," these poems cover the violence in the news, the violence in our schools, the violence in our homes, as well as the violence in our own minds. Despite the sheer amount of pain and suffering in these poems, many still make a move toward hope and redemption, such as Christopher Davis's "How Can I Turn Off This Engine Now?" where he writes "I, who, like you, feel as if being happy/is like fumbling with some other tongue./The lucky figure it out, how to forgive/this cruel world." It's evident as well in Monifa Love's short but potent "Shall We Gather at the River?" And Bob Hicok shares an unusual story in "The Bond," which explores the unexpected relationship between a man stabbed in the chest and his attacker. Even after the attacker is found dead by police, the victim refuses to ID the body and learns to love the scar that "entertains/his fingers, is kissed by the woman he loves/as birds must adore the sky, grows so deep/into memory that his body would be broken/without it."

As William Olsen writes in his disturbing poem, "Blood," "Can anyone ever make blood do anything? . . . /On and on till the questions are all open coffins." Perhaps Benjamin Alire Saénz furthers this idea in "Angel," a poem to his wife, a judge who deals in child abuse cases, which says: "I picture/You asking the hundred difficult questions that must be/Asked." It's these same questions that we must ask of ourselves, each other, everyone. It's through asking these questions and coming up with our own answers that we can go on in the face of atrocities such as Waco and Oklahoma City, or accept that people such as Jeffrey Dahmer and Ted Bundy exist. History has glamorized many of these perpetrators of violence into minor folk heroes and softened the horrors of mass violence. Charles Manson has a cult following in America after decades of incarceration. O. J. Simpson is given complimentary golf passes, airfare, rental cars, and dinners all over America. Worst of all, in a recent study of fourth-grade students at a school district in central Wisconsin, 15 percent of them don't believe that slavery was "all that bad," and nearly 10 percent of them don't believe the Holocaust really happened. We must not forget.

These poems bare the truth, hard and ugly and cold as it often is. These poems don't allow us to forget. These poems demand answers and explanations that are different than the lyrics of rap records or the rhetoric of hate-mongers. These poems are necessary. We want to be able to eat lunch and have the big news on TV and in our lives be who won the Super Bowl or who's running for president, not where was the latest school shooting or what's the name of America's newest mass murderer. Like any parents, we don't want our children growing up ignorant of history, nor do we want them growing up in a country that is no longer safe. And that's perhaps the most important reason that we put this anthology together. Let's not forget.

October 2001: We received the final page proofs for this anthology not three weeks after the terrorist attacks on the World Trade Center and the Pentagon. As writers and editors, we love it when our work is timely, but this is one occasion we wish we'd hit wide of the mark.

President George W. Bush recently declared war on international terrorism. As we bomb Afghanistan's major cities for a third time in three days, the major U.S. newspapers are reporting that America is in "significant danger" of terrorist reprisal. As in the past, perhaps literature and the creative arts — this book included — can begin the healing process and provoke a new-found appreciation for peace and harmony, unrealistic as it may seem today.

As Tim O'Brien writes in *The Things They Carried*, "Stories are for joining the past to the future. Stories are for those late hours in the night when you can't remember how you got from where you were to where you are. Stories are for eternity, when memory is erased, when there is nothing to remember except the story." The poems included in this anthology are stories that join the past to the future. Let us hope that they last, too, beyond when memory is erased, that the words ring on.

ACKNOWLEDGMENTS

We would like to thank our families for providing much-needed support during the years we spent compiling and editing this book. Our sincere thanks and heartfelt gratitude goes to Holly Carver, our wonderful editor at the University of Iowa Press, for believing that this project was as important as we knew it was. Also, and mostly, a giant thank you to all the wonderful poets who were generous not only in sharing with us their great work, but also for helping us contact and solicit poetry from kindred souls. Finally, we would like to dedicate this book to all of the people who've experienced violence of any type in their lives and let them know that this book is for them most of all.

Like Thunder

THEODICY KIM ADDONIZIO

Suppose we could see evil with such clarity we wouldn't hesitate
to stamp it out like stray sparks from a fire. Look at those boys
shooting baskets in the park, jostling each other to hook the ball
through the iron circle at the end of the asphalt — what if you knew

a secret about one of them? Shirtless, he stands vibrating
at the edge of an imaginary line, the orange globe trembling
at the tips of his fingers, sweat drawing the light into his skin —
what if he'd done something unspeakable, something I can't

talk about but know you can imagine, to the one
you love most in this world? Your child, maybe,
or the person whose body you know so well you can see it
simply by closing your eyes — What if he'd broken that body;

do you think if I handed you a gun you would walk up
to that shining boy and use it? You might think first
that maybe he couldn't help himself, maybe he was trying
as he stood there concentrating on his shot to stop the noise

of some relentless machine grinding away in his brain,
the same one you hear in yours sometimes, bearing down until
you can't tell what's true anymore, or good. Suppose God
began to have that trouble. Suppose the first man

turned out cruel and stupid, a cartoon creature
that farted and giggled continuously; suppose the woman ripped
saplings from the earth all day and refused to speak
or be grateful for anything. What if they decided to torment

the smaller, weaker beasts, and just as God was about
to strike them dead and start over they turned towards each other
and discovered fucking, and the serpent whispered *Look at them*
and God's head filled with music while the wild sparks leaped

from their bodies, bright as the new stars in the heavens?

FROM THEN TO NOW KIM ADDONIZIO

for Dorianne

I've been thinking of your father,
who stood over your bed
and casually opened you,
who walked down the hall in his robe and slippers
after lifting the childhood from your body
night after night, the way the knife
lifts the delicate skeleton of the fish
from its flesh, the way the magician
slips the scarlet silk from his black sleeve.
I didn't know you then. At seven
I was picking out my birthday doll
in a hotel gift shop, and my father
was in that other world, the one where words
and gestures drifted idly down on
threads of smoke from his cigarettes
and the smell of his cologne. I felt alone
but I did not feel that terror
of my father's step. Whenever I
see you now, I see your father, too,
standing behind your shoulder in his pajamas,
a vague grey shape, oddly humble
in his refusal to vanish. I see his hands like two
hooks descending, and when we hug in greeting
it's him I take you from,
I put my arms around that sleepy child
and make him give her back.

AMMO LIZ AHL

Tonight we talk about ammo.
Teacher lines up shells on the desk,
tallest to shortest, like Russian nesting dolls.
Some are pointy and slender.
Some are short and stout.

He names each one, affectionately.
He shows us stripper clips,
half-moon clips, full-moon clips.
He caresses the slightly curved
machine-gun magazine.
We pass around the largest shell —
a .600 Nitro Express from an elephant gun —
and the smallest — a .2 mm rimfire
used in old-fashioned gallery guns.
We feel the heft of lead shot in our palms.
We finger the sharp edges of hollow bullets.

After ammo, teacher shows us his prized matchlock.
It's about four hundred years old,
and several inches taller than its owner.
It kills him that he's never been able to fire it.

A WARRIOR'S TALE SANDRA ALCOSSER

We sat under a rotunda, so the smallest sound reverberated, came back historic. Richard told a story about hiking alone in the woods or northern California, how he found the decomposing body of a young woman. She was still alive. There were maggots crawling in her hands. She'd been raped, pushed over a cliff, and she had crawled back up with broken bones, to even ground, to be found or left to die. Richard told this story in front of Rachel. It must have been a kind of warrior's tale. A young man had broken into Rachel's apartment in the French Quarter. She moved back into the same apartment after the attack. Everyone thought her brave. The man had raped her, then stabbed her in the chest with her own butcher knife — she almost died of perforated lungs — and as he stabbed, he asked her, *will you be my sweetheart?* and she begged, *please call an ambulance*. Rachel broke down when she heard Richard's story, but she broke down in another room so that the men could not see her.

TEXAS CHAINSAW MASSACRE SHERMAN ALEXIE

What can you say about a movie so horrific
even its title scares people away?
— Stephen King

I
have seen it
and like it: The blood,
the way like *Sand Creek*
even its name brings fear,
because I am an American
Indian and have learned
words are another kind of violence.

This vocabulary is genetic.

When Leatherface crushes the white boy's skull
with a sledgehammer, brings it down again and again
while the boy's arms and legs spasm and kick wildly
against real and imagined enemies, I remember

another killing floor

in the slaughter yard from earlier in the film,
all the cows with their stunned eyes and mouths
waiting for the sledgehammer with fear so strong
it becomes a smell that won't allow escape. I remember

the killing grounds

of Sand Creek
where 105 Southern Cheyenne and Arapaho women and children
and 28 men were slaughtered by 700 heavily armed soldiers,
led by Colonel Chivington and his Volunteers. *Volunteers.*

Violence has no metaphors; it does have reveille.

Believe me there is nothing surprising
about a dead body. This is late in the 20th century
tears come easily without sense:
taste and touch have been replaced
by the fear of reprisal. I have seen it

and like it: The butchery, its dark humor
that thin line "between art and exploitation,"
because I recognize the need to prove blood
against blood. I have been in places
where I understood *Tear his heart out
and eat it whole.* I have tasted rage
and bitterness like skin between my teeth.

I have been in love.

I first saw it in the reservation drive-in
and witnessed the collected history
of America roll and roll across the screen,
voices and dreams distorted by tin speakers.

"Since then, I have been hungry
for all those things I haven't seen."

This country demands that particular sort of weakness:
we must devour everything on our plates
and ask for more. Our mouths hinge open.
Our teeth grow long and we gnaw them down
to prevent their growth into the brain. I have

seen it and like it: The blood,
the way like music
it makes us all larger
and more responsible
for our sins,
because I am an American
Indian and have learned

hunger becomes madness easily.

PROSECUTOR WILLIAM BAER

Another homicide, another trial.
He hated every single bit of it.
So why did he still bother? He seldom saw
his wife these days; his paycheck was a joke;
and the boss was nothing but a petty party hack
scheming to be governor. It also
wasn't the murder scenes, the sleazy lawyers,
soft judges, lying witnesses, and timid juries.

It also wasn't some personal vendetta
against the thugs, the whores, and all the psychopaths.
Even noble notions about "justice"
weren't enough anymore. But still, he knew why,
watching the trembling, devastated father
of the dead Hispanic girl
— battered, raped, stabbed over 25 times —
unable to hold his shaking cup of coffee.

PATRIOTICS DAVID BAKER

Yesterday a little girl got slapped to death by her daddy,
    out of work, alcoholic, and estranged two towns down river.
America, it's hard to get your attention politely.
    America, the beautiful night is about to blow up

and the cop who brought the man down with a shot to the chops
    is shaking hands, dribbling chaw across his sweaty shirt,
and pointing cars across the courthouse grass to park.
    It's the Big One one more time, July the 4th,

our country's perfect holiday, so direct a metaphor for war,
    we shoot off bombs, launch rockets from Drano cans,
spray the streets and neighbors' yards with the machine-gun crack
    of fireworks, with rebel yells and beer. In short, we celebrate.

It's hard to believe. But so help the soul of Thomas Paine,
    the entire county must be here — the acned faces of neglect,
the halter-tops and ties, the bellies, badges, beehives,
    jacked-up cowboy boots, yes, the back-up singers of democracy

all gathered to brighten in unambiguous delight
    when we attack the calm and pointless sky. With terrifying vigor
the whistle-stop across the river will lob its smaller arsenal
    halfway back again. Some may be moved to tears.

We'll clean up fast, drive home slow, and tomorrow
    get back to work, those of us with jobs, convicting the others
in the back rooms of our courts and malls — yet what
    will be left of that one poor child, veteran of no war

but her family's own? The comfort of a welfare plot,
    a stalk of wilting prayers? Our fathers' dreams come true as nightmare.
So the first bomb blasts and echoes through the streets and shrubs:
    red, white, and blue sparks shower down, a plague

of patriotic bugs. Our thousand eyeballs burn aglow like punks.
    America, I'd swear I don't believe in you, but here I am,
and here you are, and here we stand again, agape.

MORE RAIN DAVID BAKER

1.

This is all still something of a mystery.

In 1953, just after that war,
my Uncle Wayne took a wooden bootjack and whacked
my father, just once, upside his head

— to whip him
into shape,

he said.

2.

Shape for what? nobody really figured out,
or still won't say.
I was born about a year
later.

I believe
it was raining hard
when Wayne belted my father — as
it is now, again, for the umpteenth time
this drenched, green, madly
growing spring.
My father bled like a stuck pig,
to use their favorite way of recapturing the moment.

3.

Whenever the rains keep coming down floating
as they do now in the morning
in just enough cool June stillness to meet themselves
sneaking back up a foot or so
as fog,

and whenever the two sweet gum trees
stationed by my study window
bow so heavy

with the accumulated rains and their own strange,
bobbing, light green seed pods
— which seem, now that I think about it,
like those tiny
floating naval mines, spiked, deadly —
I like to think I understand the whole thing.

4.

What whole thing?

5.

My father will show you, if you ask in the right tone of voice,
the long, ragged scar just
under his right ear

and ranging like a map line
down the negotiable border of his jaw.
And in the rain especially,
and the humidity, it will stand out red, still burning.

6.

He was already married, just home from the war: hero.
And he needed, to Wayne, to be whipped.

How Wayne knew this, nobody knows.

But I guess now it's got
more than a little to do with the rains —
the easy rain shaking the grasses,
the rain slipping over everywhere from the rooftops and gutters,
the same rain, bad rain,

the constant rain soaking down the roots
until each rotted leaf lets go, pale and conquered,
the rain everywhere,

all the rain hissing and tapping and clouding the day,

the rain,
which has fallen much too much this spring,

7.

and can drive you so crazy
you'll do just about anything

to kill it.

HATE CRIME BARRY BALLARD

She spun on the apex of her fragile
morality, screaming like the last breath
that can't find an explanation. And death
wasn't forgiving with its waste and vile
display that colored her hands as they filled
themselves with what memory she could compress
into this narrowing ache. And the rest
of her life emptied where the blood was spilled.

And she imagined that her son stood up
from the history still left in his body,
asking to finish the life he'd begun.
Concrete shook beneath her, and lightning struck
from street lights as she folded restlessly,
without room for the officer's questions.

FOR ROLAND, PRESUMED TAKEN JIM BARNES

By the time we missed you dusk was settling in.
The first reaction was to think
of drowning, the deep hole just north of the house
that the spring flows into
out from under the sycamore.
You had played there earlier in the day
and had wanted to wade the still water
after minnows schooling the shadows.

We tracked you back to the spring, and I died
with fear that you would be floating
among the lilies, white as the ghost of fish.
But your tracks veered left
toward the valley where the cattle grazed,
then vanished in the flowing grass.
I blew the horn that called the cattle in.
You knew the sound and loved the way
the cattle came loping up at feeding time.

Roland, still, today, you cannot hear the sound of the horn,
cannot holler back up the mountainside
to let us know in your wee voice you are safe and found.
Why you walked off into the green of that day
we can never know, except the valley
and the mountain beyond must have yielded a sudden
sound or flash of light that took your eyes away.
And you were gone. It is as if

eagles swooped you up, leaving
not one trace to tell us the way you went away.
Nights I imagine the beat of drums,
the clanging of toy swords,
rocking horses neighing
on their tracks.
In another age
I would offer
up my glove
to God
to have you back.

Now, we have packed away your life
in boxes we store
in case the memory
we hold is swept away
by chance
or the slow years.

THE MEN WHO KILLED MY BROTHER

EDWARD BARTÓK-BARATTA

Behind the left ear a scar
shaped like the hand of a priest lifted

to bestow a blessing, a small
neat mustache like many men

standing in a row, where
you, me, a friend's sister

might point and say *That one*, and from there
his right to remain silent

began. The second carried himself
like a boat far from water, too

large for a man, the size of an average
desk turned on its side. My memory

makes him a lover of pizza, sour cream and butter
plopped down and running

from a potato, that vegetable shape
not unlike his own. The third I would have

a drained, green bottle, a cracked
clay pot with begonias, the anonymous

tan ruler made of cheap pine — shape, voice,
texture and odor

beyond my knowing, my extended
day in the desert, my mind a violent

sea before the calm. Living,
and suffering like my brother, Murderers,

have I forgotten
to thank or to forgive you?

BEARING WITNESS ELLEN BASS

for Jacki

If you have lived it, then
It seems I must hear it.
— Holly Near

When the long-fingered leaves of the sycamore
flutter in the wind, spiky
seed balls swinging, and a child throws his aqua
lunch bag over the school yard railing, the last thing,
the very last thing you want to think about
is what happens to children when they're crushed
like grain in the smooth mortar of the cruel.

We weep at tragedy, a baby sailing
through the windshield like a cabbage, a shoe.
The young remnants of war, arms sheared and eyeless,
they lie like eggs on the rescue center's bare floor.

But we draw a line at the sadistic,
as if our yellow plastic tape would keep harm
confined. We don't want to know
what generations of terror do to the young
who are fed like cloth
under the machine's relentless needle.

In the paper, we'll read about the ordinary neighbor
who chopped up boys; at the movies we pay
to shoot up that adrenaline rush —
and the spent aftermath, relief
like a long-awaited piss.

But face to face with the living prey,
we turn away, rev the motor, as though
we've seen a ghost — which, in a way, we have:
the one who wanders the world,
tugging on sleeves, trying to find the road home.

And if we stop, all our fears
will come true. The knowledge of evil
will coat us like grease

from a long shift at the griddle.
We'll breathe it in — a speck of uranium
ticking in our blood. Algae smothering a lake,
it will choke our dreams. Our sweat
will smell like the sweat of the victims.

And this is why you do it — listen
at the outskirts of what our species
has accomplished, listen until the world is flat
again, and you are standing on its edge.
This is why you hold them in your arms, allowing
their snot to smear your skin, their sour
breath to mist your face. You listen
to slash the membrane that divides us, to plant
the hard shiny seed of yourself
in the common earth. You crank
open the rusty hinge of your heart
like an old beach umbrella. You ratchet
open your body like giving birth. Because God
is not a flash of diamond light. God is
the kicked child, the child
who rocks alone in the basement,
the one fucked so many times
she does not know her name, her mind
burning like a star.

THE ADOLESCENT SUICIDE JILL BIALOSKY

The girl
walks carefully over the tracks
her head raised to the sun
in this city where houses
painted in cheap colors sag.
No well-tended healthy lawns to view
from the furniture-
less porches. Buds ready to bloom
on the depressed, twisted trees.
What replaces the magnificent lights
in the mind when it goes dark
behind the capitol and courthouse
and this city to nowhere sparkles?

In this city
of her birth, she must have walked
back and forth hundreds of times through the downtown
intersection looking for the road less traveled,
past the local Chinese restaurant, a pub, Jack's, the fancy sea-house,
rubbing her free hand along a cornice of a building, a brick,
ear turned to hear, the way a small boy puts his hand
to the tracks to feel the vibrations
of an oncoming train before crossing
to the other side.

Metallic,
industrial sky, between concrete slabs
the crocuses show off their yellow crowns.
What is it that draws her? Is it colder or warmer there?
What whistle beckons?
Her brown skin. Her elegant walk,
as if no one on earth mattered.
Does the air smell different
when we are shut out from sight?

I read once
that when a suicide is ready
to die the light goes out of her eyes.
The day the great aunt, lover of daughters,
took the suicide to lunch,
her blue eyes without light looked dim, gray,

vacant, like a house without windows, a tree
without the life force. A girl without hope.
A story without a legend.

   I can just imagine it,
the girl at the table, sorrow-
less, clear and cognizant,
no longer prisoner to love's
illusion of un-loneliness,
the choice having already been made.
For once, her mind un-
encumbered by complication,
deliberate, without appetite,
to please the great aunt,
the beloved orders her last meal.
A turkey sandwich. Pickle on the side. Diet Coke.

VIOLENCE WENDY BISHOP

Your daughter is dead.
During the lost hours

When she leaves the house
And the car is found later

Engine running, the light on
And the door open, entrance

And exit making the same gesture,
And the search's finale a day

Later, you fail backwards
Through a life that had its starting

And its ending within your
Head-shaking knowledge.

The day you went to a countryside
Auction: the straw-strewn floor, buggies

And board benches, jumble of pine
Hutches, entire households

Piled high in a dark tunneling
of wood-oiled indoor corridors.

Your little girl slipped away,
Pulled a hand like a leaf fluttering

Gaily from a brittle fall tree.
At your alarm, your husband cornered

The auctioneer. You ran to one door
And another, calling out for her

And staring into the summer sun
That thrust its sheaves onto the planking

Of the porch. Your heart was melting —
A pewter bullet-mold — taking the shape

Of a deadly weapon, and then her answer,
Her unforgivable happiness of escape

And high laughter. You held her all the way
Home saying: never, never, never.

Now, years later, the state trooper
Has a soft-brimmed hat, eyes that dip

To a winter hard ground as if tracing
The slow cinema of a disaster. Where?

You ask. When? How? And he gives
The fearful answer. Men, you think,

Men do this. And your gun-metal gray
Heart remembers, your husband telling you

About a man in Chicago who kept three women
Captive. One escaped and reported

The man and a room full of body parts,
And you told him never to say such things

Again at your breakfast table. Surprised
He nodded his answer as the trooper nods.

And you know it's not just men
And it's not just you, waiting,

For your son and husband come to you:
Each embrace is long. Each loss is large.

EVIDENCE OF DEATH'S VOODOO — INSIDE AND OUTSIDE THE "GUN AS ART EXHIBIT" WENDY BISHOP

I'm in black leather, the guns are wrapped in string, tape, wire, and cloth.

WWII, my mother worked in a munitions factory.

Klansman holds his gun like a broadsword.

After watching *The Essential Beatles* video, my thirteen-year-old is desolate. "I wish they'd get back together," she says.

Women with guns: Gail with a .45 caliber Colt Gold Cup; Libby with her 380 Sigsaur.

Sometimes the flat dull gunmetal dumbness of it all gets to me.

Under an illustration: "Dick said, 'Stop Jane, don't touch the gun.'" — *"happiness is a warm gun . . . .*

Mornings, I gulp premarin and prozac, cognitive Molotov cocktail.

At lunch, at the mall, we all order chicken fingers and joke about human fingers.

Photo caption: "I'm gonna beat you like a stepchild."

Somewhere, someone makes it his business to manufacture POLICE EVIDENCE tape and POLICE EVIDENCE tags.

bang, bang, shoot, shoot" —

Theoretical bullet trajectories: through a banana; through an apple; through a headless, human torso.

Termites. A friend suggests I paint each with the name of an enemy before I call in the exterminators.

So help me. At the thought of this. I laugh.

AIM BRUCE BOND

What child could resist the sweet sting
it fired into things, that ecstasy of glass,
how floodlights chipped and sputtered
when we cracked them, blackening over the dead street.

This was the future, a deeper euphoria
than cigarettes or money, however slight
our chances with such a minor rifle
and any but the most breakable of lives.

Our incompetence was mercy, the way it spared us
our little cruelties. And overhead
the question of our highest misses, if
they turned dangerous under the stars, falling.

How a gun loves a living target — any boy
will tell you — so I picked a sparrow,
a measly bird, yet when magnified
you could see it perched on a power wire,

the tiny black blisters of its gaze,
a pulse barely perceptible in its throat.
A part of me thought I'd never hit it
and still doesn't. Just as I fix it

in memory's scope, one eye closed,
the other locked in its circle, the bird
slips safely from the rifle's cross.
If I rush with giddy horror to the shuddering

feathers, at the end they disappear.
And in that moment as I fall away
from the world, I am wedded to it
and want nothing more than to give life

back through some slash in its fabric,
to walk straight as a bullet into the dead,
becoming radiant, necessary,
safer in their body than my own.

IMPROPER DISPOSAL JOHN BRADLEY

for Ellen Franklin

The words suggest illegal
dumping of a bloodstained
mattress or mound of toxic soil.
Not a baby, wrapped
in a woman's sweater, left
on the steps of a church
in weather cold enough to freeze
a bottle of wine. Why
would anyone leave
a baby like this? The police
want to speak to the mother
because the father . . . he could be
anyone and no one, a boy
who can't remember where
he left his sperm, or a cloud
of voices in the form of a dove.

"Intrauterine asphyxia"
states the Cook County medical
examiner's office for cause
of death. The baby stillborn
making the mother not a murderer
but a parent who simply wanted
a Christian burial for her child.
Though she's still guilty
of "improper disposal of a body."
"In her own way, she was caring
for her child," notes the pastor
of the church. "That's no sin."
Sin, in a land where one in five
children go to bed hungry,
is something more
common, less newsworthy.

THE DARK SIDE OF DAZZLE SEAN BRENDAN-BROWN

Her children fill toy ships, await dawn's majestic
laser show. A physicist, she warns them of light's
deleterious penetrations. The children sing, manipulate
pale hands over complete faces. Their shadow-tigers

devour three squirrels. They cry "feed us"
until she distributes crescents from her purse.
Rhododendrons catch some crumbs. The children fire
crusts at a bum, morsels reach his sparrow-brown beard.
"Thank you, children," he laughs with them, pushing
bread into his mouth. Morning hesitates,

light thickens, he chews. His knife's
stag-handled and brass-riveted
with carbon-steel serrated
to saw through any bones struck. "Stop now, no,"
the woman scolds, folding herself over the park bench.

The sparrow splits her fat suede purse,
drags lipstick stripes down his forehead. The children
whimper. "Hush! I'll buy you ice cream." He shows them
her money then abandons them, walks stropping the knife
against his thighs. The children, stomachs full of
bread, drowse as the sun strikes everything
with tardy fury.

ESSAYS ON EXCESS AND ESCAPE GAYLORD BREWER

1. Feeding off the Corpse

We loaf and lounge, usual intolerance
mollified by luxurious gluttony.
There's blubber enough for everybody, children
will grow noticeably in days, adults add an inch
of good fat. We're even generous
with the tour boats. Let'm have
a photograph. Here we lie, bathing in it,
one creature's misfortune a smorgasbord for all.
Life lesson number one.

Feel how that oil feels on fur. Holy Jesus!
Smell that fetid sweetness. You say it won't last?
Watch us while it does: we're eating.

2. Style

Hang up the wife, put her away with coats.
Kiss the baby — sweet dimple buttocks,
pink marshmallow arms, simple brutal
mistake. Fold it up with the bath towels.

They adore, adore, adore you.
Leave that, too, rolled with your stupid socks.

Now: paint on that best suit of blood.
Wiggle your ass in a bone yard,
grab fifty chin-ups under barb wire,
moonlight, and smoke. Then border towns,

a private howling closet all your own,
and one last hour to murder, linger, and destroy.

LITTLETON MICHAEL BUGEJA

The schoolyard tolls as once the graveyard did
For trenchcoat Thomas Gray, whose madding crowd
Secured the gates of mercy. Now we heed

The cable aftermath of talking heads
Advising us to *hire more armed guards*,
To *lose illegal guns*. Bulletins bombard

The internet and cheapen the debate
About the role of Hollywood and hate
Until the circus folds the tent and goes

When coverage of Columbine plateaus
With Kosovo. The images of that
Seem similar, the eerie *"rat-tat-tat"*

Of clips accompanied by audio
Of real ones, to which we have since Waco
Grown accustomed on TV as stimulus:

Littleton will slip into unconsciousness
Of information-angst and from our minds.
We've learned to fear a future that rewinds

By click of mouse, by button of remote,
Transmitting terror live by satellite,
Though some of us remember history

When news was truth and not reality.

SHOOTER RULES MICHAEL BUGEJA

The millimeters of your life are nine.
The caliber is larger than your age.
The drug of choice is your adrenaline.
The victim can be smaller than the gauge.

A chamber has no doors, and yet revolves.
An automatic takes a clip, not gears.
You don't show up in court. You are absolved:
A case contains propellant now, not beer.

You don't subscribe, you load a magazine.
Your bullets here have talons, not the birds.
The only nests above are submachine.
Your silencer speaks louder than your words.

Rounds go off, the cops no longer make them.
You invent the rules, but cannot break them.

I'm mad, and I don't mean deranged, rabid, foolish, imprudent, infatuated, or wildly frivolous. No, I'm angry with America. That's where I live.

I'm anonymous, poor, single, educated, an immigrant and a woman raising my child alone. Oh, I know what you'll say. Something like "Well,

if she doesn't like it here, she can go back to where she comes from. Ha! Maybe it's better over there." I said I live here. You don't listen to me.

He's mad, and here I mean provoked, irritated, irrational, impetuous, and frustrated with adults. He's an American kid. Helpless, average, middle-class,

lonely. So, what do you say about that? You say nothing. You didn't even notice the kid. He's just a kid. Kids are weird these days. Some of them pierce

their eyebrows, noses, lips, tongues, belly buttons, nipples and tattoo the back of their calves, necks, skulls, around their limbs. They dye their hair in black,

orange, purple, green. They bound. No beads and flowers. "Kids aren't doing anything I haven't done when it comes to drugs and alcohol," you think.

They're dead. They were kids in high school, girls, boys, rich, poor, middle-class, conservative, liberal, without political opinion, with two

parents, one, or none. Some wore trench coats. Are you listening to me? You don't know why kids would blow up their school and

fire on their peers at random. You're speechless. The world is crazy, not you. You're fed up with kids. You can't wait to send yours back to daycare,

school, after-school program, lock-ins, summer camp, church camp, boot camp. More dead. They were kids in a church, I'm not sure how they were.

I hear what you say. If you're a politician running for President and you need money, you grab a little girl in your arms, give her a kiss

on the cheek, and say something like, "Evil is on America." So, what do you do about gun control? Nothing. America is a free country.

I say, "You're going to let people kill each other?" But you don't listen to me because I'm anonymous, poor, educated, an immigrant and a woman raising my child alone, and I don't go to church. I've said I live in America and I'm mad. You don't like what I say. You don't have to please me. How

could I hurt you with my words? You don't believe in education. You pray. You're greedy. You're smart, efficient, powerful, rich, and you're the boss.

If you're a TV producer, you have people filming, commenting, interviewing, giving me a break from all the death with weather, business, sports, Hollywood,

and fashion reports. You track the history of mass murdering all the way to C. J. Whitman and the Tower shooting in 1966. You try to lull me.

I'm not a Texan. Why should I care? You have people say, "People can do bad things. They're not crazy. They're just men." I agree

with you. You see, you're the men who have transformed other men into creatures addicted to commercials, soap operas, guns, bazookas, bombs,

murders, speed, movie stars, pop stars, and sport stars. They go crazy, but you don't. You have the cash and the cookies. You do bad things.

LITHIUM MARCUS CAFAGÑA

I think of my brother and his routine:
the cellblock lights, the TV turned on
or off by schedule, the amber vials
in the infirmary cabinet,

the pills he can't forget or he sleepwalks
into walls, shaves his Vandyke
down to a fascist patch below the nostrils.
The sedan parked him at the bank

where he stood with the ski mask, the alarm.
But the gun he waved was loaded
only with pellets, the getaway car
rented under his name. When he

and I spread our fingers on either side
of the Plexiglas, I ask him
how he could do something that stupid.
He confesses through the food slot

that he wanted some fast cash to fix the crushed
white door of his Dodge Dart so his date
wouldn't have to squeeze behind the wheel
and scootch herself across the seat.

IN A MOTEL IN LOUISIANA I WATCH THE PIRATES AND THE OJ SIMPSON FREEWAY CHASE AT THE SAME TIME

RICK CAMPBELL

Stan Musial meets the Emperor of Japan
as OJ with his gun to his head
is driven down the LA freeway
nine cop cars following, choppers above,
and NBC's cameras live, showing us a white
Bronco in a solitary parade, as if the mere
image of his car on a freeway was news and
everyone is worried that OJ might shoot
himself as the cops show more restraint
than they showed Rodney King
or than OJ showed his wife
and just then the Pirates turn a sweet
double play. The Emperor and his wife
don't cheer, maybe out of deference
to their host. Maybe they aren't fans. Stan
the Man stays in the shadows at the rear
of the luxury box so we don't know if he
curses the Cardinal batter who could
not lay off the sinker low and away.

VOYEUR SANDRA CASTILLO

for Hillary Russell

I watch you through my small window
though black wrought-iron and rain separate us
like a thin layer of plasma.
Wet, tangled hair,
you move in silence through violent air,
breathe in, oxygen blue.
Face flushed red, skin, vein-blue,
a ghost suffocating in the outline of night.

My lips part, make no sound.
I want to tell you that you can write yourself
out of the tight spaces of your life,
that it isn't true;
we do not have to marry men like our fathers,
live lives like our mothers,
watch them unfold
out of the celluloid closet
of ambiguous thought.

We can break clean, Hil, free.

But he is there, wet, breathless;
alcohol fills him, spills forth.
I move for you,
wave my arms to save you
though I cannot touch the space you occupy,
for I am audience in this dream
that moves across the dark screens of my lids
and you stand in the distance,
out of range, out of focus.

IN THE SEASON OF SUICIDES   LISA D. CHAVEZ

she slides her finger
across the barrel of a gun again.
She finds it beautiful: its snout
gray blue and pleasing,
the mechanism's smooth mesh
and movement as she draws
the chamber back. Now the barrel
rests in her mouth, the taste familiar
as her own blood. It is March,
but the earth is still rigid
with winter, the sky blue,
but cold as a marble slab.

It is the season of suicides.
Last month her neighbor
exploded like a star, ignition
sparked by a single shotgun shell.
He was twenty-two. And though
they'd never spoken, she recalls
his long reddish hair, how he'd wave
as she drove past, one hand held high
above his head. She never knew
his name. And her sister, too,
the body in the bathtub, the brown
plastic bottle submerged in the liquid
chill. But her they brought back.

Night drops like a curtain
on a stage. She mixes another drink,
settles in her chair. At her feet,
the dead neighbor's dog sighs
in its sleep. She thinks of herself,
images flashing past
like still photos on a screen.
She used to be strong.
Split her own wood. Lived
alone. She pictures herself
in her shooting class, legs planted,
blonde braid hanging straight down
her back as she raised her arms
to aim. She was a good shot.

At the range, the middle-aged men
used to eye her and smile.

Another picture clicks
into place. Her sister.
My sister is weak, she thinks.
Vodka and sleeping pills,
or the razor's red dance
along her wrists. Never quite
enough. Three attempts in two years,
didn't stop the husband
from filing the divorce.

There is no reason, really.
Yes, a man left her too,
but that was months past.
Still pain squats on her
chest like an incubus,
its breath sour, numbing and gray.
All winter she has existed,
slumped in this chair, and listened
to the fire's voice, to the darkness
settling heavily around the house.
The pistol comforting
on her thigh.

And now the nights
are shorter. Now summer beckons
like a young man waving.
But she is tired of it all: the cabin
she built herself, her sister's needy calls
at 3 A.M., the way shadow
gives way to light. She snaps the clip
into the gun, and the dog
jerks awake. Watches. In her mind,
a brilliant red peony
bursts into bloom.

THE NEWS MAXINE CHERNOFF

On hearing
that twelve
children
die
by handguns
each day
in the U.S.A.,
my son,
aged six,
says, "I'm
glad we
don't
live there."

GOING POSTAL PAUL CHRISTENSEN

My neighbor cruises with a lug wrench on his lap;
he's into road rage. He hopes the guy behind
will pick a fight. He's ready.
Ready as any kid with a semi-automatic
looking for a playground. They're going postal.

My girlfriend's got a mace gun
big as a potato on her keychain;
she likes to flash it in my face
when we're on a date. I don't get frantic,
I just laugh. And then we both go postal.

We never talk, we drop some speed
and vibrate in the mosh pit, bodies spinning
all around us, overhead. Kids are outside
smoking crack and laughing, bashing
windshields just to see if they can bleed.

We're going postal. It's cool to lose control,
to let it happen. You don't know where it ends,
you just keep moving. And when the world
is spinning upside down, you're going postal.
Postal is running around without a head.

NEWBORN FOUND ALIVE IN
SHALLOW GRAVE DAVID CITINO

After that first birth
    out of the soothe of dark,
I was a groan, a bruise, eyes

clenched like fists against the light.
    Having been abused down a tunnel
tight enough to flatten a head,

narrowest way in the world,
    fontanel tickling out my panic,
I was handled harshly

in the mother country, land
    of the loud, unsterile, dry.
I noticed I was naked, heard

the sob and gasp of shame
    that canceled out her childhood.
Out of her mind with me,

she rushed to put me back
    in the dark where only she
could feel my furtive song,

the dirge of one tiny heart.
    I hear the rooting and snort
of the frenzied dogs of evening,

human feet padding behind.
    Once again the mortal dance,
panting struggle upward.

I drag the wet scarlet cord
    no longer tethering this body
to ever. Such howling.

I move to touch the rising moon.

IN THE BEDROOM OF FEAR DAVID CITINO

The world is to run from, my child.
Here, for example, on this pretty card
you can press in a holy book, the one
come to save you from eternal fire,
vile sins of Mother and Dad.
He's having a little problem.
Blood runs in his eyes from the crown
of thorns hammered onto his head
by the police. He was framed.
He'll be nailed, stretched on a cross
so all the world can count his ribs,
ooh and aah over the carnival
of wounds. But don't worry.
He loves you. His followers
will have eyes pulled out,
breasts sawn off, testicles crushed
slowly — special effects worse than
the first hour of *Saving Private Ryan*.
Faith, the world calls this.
And that's not the half of it.
Listen to the armies scurrying across
the base-boards as you try
to sleep, roiling on closet floor, a tangle
of gooey tentacles, mandibles,
tireless ovipositors. — Hey,
who's that peering through the blinds
as you try to sleep? And the worst
is yet to come: even now
something beyond imagining
is stirring beneath your sheets.
Good night. Sleep tight.
(Don't let the bed-bugs bite.)

KACZYNSKI JEFFREY CLAPP

There was something poignant in
that photo of your house,
wrapped and traveling south
on the Interstate:
shack in a pack,
"House on the Go" by Christo.
It settled through the Midwest
like a bad dream.
On "News of the Week"
the analyst's lip curled
when he discerned its loathsome shape:
angular and black
more of an over-sized outhouse
than any respectably American abode.
At every Motel 6, the driver slept
beside his load.

And what about you, Kaczynski?
Dread's poster boy
aging counter-culture freak
forsaking the umbrella
of university and over-weening corporation
for atomic mushrooms of the imagination
nurtured in rural isolation —
not one who couldn't reach,
one who chose not to go.
You could almost do it in '73 —
shut off the newspapers and the TV
outlast the draft
baptize yourself in the blood
of backwoods hippie religion
grown in the rural backyards
of West Virginia, Vermont and Tennessee,
splintery steps where babies nursed
on L'il Abner breasts
and parents drank Red Zinger tea
ate soy curd and buckwheat grouts
and fried chicken in joints downtown
boiling water for home-cured ham
and fat babies born
to beaded hippies on the lam

as straggly stalks of cannabis
flowered in the corn
until
browsing through TIME magazine one day
they saw themselves suddenly removed
cultural sun setting on funky paradise
tie-dyed T-shirts no longer relevant
or tippy VW vans
music turning disco
poetry gone slam
Welcome Wall Street, re-uptake
inhibitors and gourmet food
capitalism turning glamorous
socialism, crude

and Ted, what about you?

alive but not well in Montana
nursing the fungus in your socks
cave dweller on some forgotten
island off Guam
lost soldier of the last civil war
carving your own tormented features
into some private Mt. Rushmore
keeping notebooks for J. Edgar Hoover to read
packing death for strangers
to open and bleed
those men whose jobs you might have had
(*techno-whores!*)
their own last mornings
no worse than yours

2212 WEST FLOWER STREET MICHAEL COLLIER

When I think of the man who lived in the house
behind ours and how he killed his wife
and then went into his own backyard,
a few short feet from my bedroom window,
and put the blue-black barrel of his 30.06
inside his mouth and pulled the trigger,
I do not think about how much of the barrel
he had to swallow before his fingers reached the trigger,
nor the bullet that passed out the back of his neck,
nor the wild orbit of blood that followed
his crazy dance before he collapsed in a clatter
over the trash cans, which woke me.

Instead I think of how quickly his neighbors restored
his humanity, remembering his passion
for stars which brought him into his yard
on clear nights, with a telescope and tripod,
or the way he stood in the alley in his rubber boots
and emptied the red slurry from his rock tumblers
before he washed the glassy chunks of agate
and petrified wood. And we remembered, too,
the goose-neck lamp on the kitchen table
that burned after dinner and how he worked
in its bright circle to fashion flies and lures.
The hook held firmly in a jeweler's vise,
while he wound the nylon thread around the haft
and feathers. And bending closer to the light,
he concentrated on tying the knots, pulling them tight
against the coiled threads. And bending closer still,
turning his head slightly toward the window,
his eyes lost in the dark yard, he took the thread ends
in his teeth and chewed them free. Perhaps he saw us
standing on the sidewalk watching him, perhaps he didn't.
He was a man so much involved with what he did,
and what he did was so much of his loneliness,
our presence didn't matter. No one's did.
So careful and precise were all his passions,

he must have felt the hook with its tiny barbs
against his lip, sharp and trigger-shaped.
It must have been a common danger for him —

the wet clear membrane of his mouth threatened
by the flies and lures, the beautiful enticements
he made with his own hands and the small loose
thread ends which clung to the roof of his mouth
and which he tried to spit out like an annoyance
that would choke him.

RIGHTS MARTHA COLLINS

He had no rights, they beat him up, you've got
no right, he said, and he was right, we thought,
we saw them beat him up, right? it happened right
over there, but it was proper form, the jury
said, and they were right, if you could judge
the beating by what happened next, our driver
said, right off they up and burn the place,
this rights stuff goes too far, next thing it's an-
imal rights, vegetable rights, mow 'em down
I say, he said and turned, he had the right
of way, license to get where he needed to go,
but what if they stopped him anyway, they're
the law and that's their right, the right side
of the body's on the other side of the heart.

ARSON NICOLE COOLEY

for Elizabeth

From the porch, the world beyond
   this house rises in flame, blaze
      of stalks, trees scorched

with light. Each new crop
   is a brush fire under a sky
      black and deep as the water

when you and I stand at the river
   together, matches scratching
      our wrists, hands shaking

as we spell out unhappiness
   on our bodies
      with a gleaming blade.

Once the past closed over
   our heads like that dark
      water. It could drown us.

Pennsylvania Search & Rescue trucks
   slide past this town,
      along the highway,

to the fires men have lit
   to burn their friends', their neighbors'
      barns to dust in yellow fields.

Once, the Mississippi's flat
   surface spins images —
      I watch you trace a line

across your wrist. I watch us hurt
   ourselves before the world
      can damage our bodies.

Now your small daughter
   has your face, your hair.
      Keep her safe from that past,

from the flame's edge we
    were always drawn to.
        On Lancaster farms,

a match snags straw,
    a family blows into smoke.
        In New Orleans

old fires glitter in the grass.
    We drink until our throats
        burn. Sharp edges catch

the light while two girls rise
    to the sky's black
        chalkboard, offering them-

selves to be erased. Stay here. Stay with me.

Now let's set childhood burning.

INCANTATION PETER COOLEY

I am in prayer! I tell myself tonight,
my body returning me from my fall
through windows in myself I never saw
a way out of until this minute.
And now I'm back and still alive.
I wish I could tell you the Christmas music
carried me on wings a few seconds back
looping through Day-Glow wreathes and Santa Claus
who appeared every few feet above the door of each shop,
a tiny god the shoppers looked up to as they passed.
I wish I could tell you I was only trembling
because it was Christmas Eve, when I would be received
by my wife and children in an hour, protected,
and be at home in myself with them
whose warming breath would take me in.
This would, yes, come to pass, but for the moment
which is this poem I am only grateful
the star had come and stood, cocked above my head
and passed me over: a salesclerk with a .38
had opened fire on children queuing up
to whisper last minute wishes in St. Nick's ear.
They are all dead; their little bodies like game birds
all six spread out, then carted off by three janitors
now scrubbing down the blood-streaked floor.
Who am I praying for, the dead or me or passersby
who have no reason to be among the living
any more than you, reader, or the man, handcuffed, gagged
who may be loose within a year to surprise one of us
but not me, we think, mumbling the old words
as I did, beginning this, words catching on the tongue
and if we're lucky, invoking someone.

CITYSCAPE MARY CROW

You'll always arrive at this same city.
— Cavafy

This city where they raped and beat you
till your face was shapeless, so swollen the technician
couldn't even X ray you. What was your crime?
Walking along the highway at night because your car
broke down? Being a woman?

Yes, you had arrived at this same city, the city
you always seemed to return to, going around
in a circle, and those men had no known motive,
belonged to no death squad. Why did you return?
The buildings were the same concrete

as other cities'. No one ever seemed
to clean the paper-littered streets,
and the park grass had been plucked
by geese. Impossible to sit down.
Well, you had no other home.

Everything you touched fell apart,
yet you hadn't damaged it and you couldn't mend it.
Now what is left? The police wait at your bedside
to ask you who did it, when, how, why.
Your voice breaks through the bandages:

What city is this? Who did they think I was?

HERE AND NOW ROBERT DANA

The Japanese yen's gone
soft, and the Nikkei's
falling, the radio says.
And one murder in every
eight, back in my old
home state, Massachusetts,
is a woman or a child.
I lift from its box
the black cast iron
blossom of the hibachi;
its cheap wooden feet;
its one dozen plus one
perfectly machined and
shining nuts and bolts.
If you come here, avoid
the easy question. You
don't even know my name;
the name my mother plucked
from a Cambridge street;
name of a movie actress;
name of a tribe of Greeks.
What's history consist of?
This morning. The summer-
long march of fiddleheads
to the eroded creek-bank.
The thin, presidential
shadow of money threaded
through everything we do.
A boy already ruined
and made stupid by death
and grief and betrayal,
I remember the gilded
and pinched and downcast
faces of Boston women.
Understand it? Can you
read the mumble of the river?
The scribble of swallows
on the slick air? God
in whom I no longer believe,
I believe in this pliers

and screwdriver; in this
hibachi and its little
lotus of fire. I believe
in this. Here. And now.

HARD-BOILED EGG JIM DANIELS

Sitting at the bar
he rubbed his bald head smooth.
Bought drinks to douse his short fuse
with gasoline. Mr. Firecracker Cherry-Bomb.
Mr. One-Punch. Mr. Ass-Kicking
Mother-Fucking Dude.

Closing time, he headed out to rain and gravel.
Two young punks tripped him.
He stood and swung wild at shadows —
took a knee in the stomach and puked.
They waited, laughing, then beat him purple.

He'd cussed the kid in front of his girlfriend.
Kid came back with a brother to have some fun
with the *old red-neck pot-bellied lard-ass.*

At the bar, he'd rubbed his bald head smooth.
His hand calmly peeled an egg.
Blood in his stool — *fool killing yourself,*
doctor said. He scratched his ear as if he
didn't hear. He poured a shot in his beer
and watched it disappear.

Layers of an egg: shell, white, yolk.
He tapped it against the bar gently,
one thing he did gently. *We settle
things ourselves around here*
he always said, the threat veiled
in flimsy rags, his belly's sag.

He'd beat that manslaughter rap years ago.
This time the old gunfighter
had a fat sausage in his holster
for those hungry kids.

What had it gotten him? The black eye
of an ex-wife, two kids who chewed
his bitter name. A broken hand,
six weeks off work. The job with wrenches,
the job with brooms, every boss

out to get him. Sitting at the bar,
is it any wonder he'd rubbed
his bald head smooth? He poked
a greasy finger into an egg,
he wheezed his greasy breath
through a cigarette.
He patted his gut. *Closing time*:
He swallowed the egg, took
a last swig to kill the yellow taste.

He was big, and wasn't that
reason enough to be mean?
He smiled, the night over,
another quiet victory after all —
he'd put that young one
in his place. He rubbed
his bald head smooth and pushed
the shells into a pile
pushed himself off the stool
trying to remember the weather
outside — was it cold? How old
were his kids? Would his car start?
Wasn't he a badass mother fucker?

In the shadow of floodlights
a pine tree spikes up three stories
near the roof of the crumbling
apartment building across the street.

Below, a young couple
mother-fucks each other up
and down the block, thundering
into our darkened rooms.

Some slam windows, others
pretend to sleep through it.
I let the storm in, staring,
hands on the window ledge.
Someone call the police,

she screams, *before he kills me.*
She pulls away, then he's chasing her.
Once, I might have stepped out
to try and break it up.

The thought of a gun freezes me
in the hallway. At least
he hasn't hit her yet. My heart, stone
heavy with shame, plunges in my chest.

I flick off the light near the phone
and stand darkly watching them,
prickly like that pine,
shivering like that pine.

JOJO'S CHRISTOPHER DAVIS

The night my brother was stabbed,
but not quite stabbed to death,
I was drinking wine in a coffeeshop
called Jojo's with some friends.
He'd been walking home drunk
from a party. Two guys who'd shared a case
of beer had picked him up.
After stabbing him, they threw him
down into a canyon. Parasites
kept his wounds clean: two days later,
he climbed out. He was
found at the side of the road by
two guys. He would not let them
touch him. On May 1st,
he died in the hospital.

I've forgotten if I had a good time that night
with my friends. I probably did.
We were all in a band together.
A month later, I
left that town to go to college.
The rest of them moved too, I think.
No: on a trip home at Christmas
I saw Nancy at Jojo's. (They had
found my phone number in his pocket.)
I don't know what
was said, if we did talk.

HOW CAN I TURN OFF THIS ENGINE NOW?

CHRISTOPHER DAVIS

This evening, fear and grief grabbed me again.
Watering round evergreens out here, in front
of our ranchhouse, I surprised those two boys,

that redheaded brat, my murdered brother,
and that shuffling, sneering thug,
that Chicano who knifed Ben,

giggling on my station wagon's front seat,
diddling with the dashboard clock, fiddling
with the radio I guess I had left booming.

I lobbed rocks toward the cracked windshield.
They laughed. I screamed, "Split!" They laughed.
I shuffled inside, praying they would go home.

Later, I needed to pick up my holy father
at the airport. I delayed, a sad Atlas
moping in an orbit around the kitchen,

eating bitter leftovers out of a coffee mug,
shoulders shrugging under the glowing ceiling,
a headache angel screaming, "Die, die!" in my skull.

I craved scraping that fluorescent light off of me.
It made my white skin feel too cold.
They're still out there, that murderer

and that bloody-haired teen angel, outside
this car, jeering at me tucked down cowering
inside it, arrested behind this wheel,

helpless to abandon the front door I left unlocked.
How can I switch off this engine now? I can't rise
from this womb, shiver out there, come back in alive,

leave. This is hell. I got no choice.
Crazy mad, I shepherd that redhead
around the cul-de-sac driveway.

His gentle profile turned screaming to me,
his opened mouth smiling as he's sucked down
into that black grave under my headlights,

his cage snapping loudly under my black tires,
he cries for the mercy he can't get from me,
I who never gave myself mercy after he died,

I, who, like you, feel as if being happy
is like fumbling with some other tongue.
The lucky figure it out, how to forgive

this cruel world.

ARBORETUM ALISON HAWTHORNE DEMING

Walking to cure myself of the gun-proud
cabbie who brought me here — purple azalea,
camellias, pink rhododendron, falling
in a storm of flowers — the government
his enemy, to blame for lack of morals
because parents are arrested, their guns
taken if they discipline their children,
I find a Japanese cherry in full bloom
though its foot-thick trunk is scarred
with a healing gash that spirals
from the ground up the bark to
where the wood narrows branching
to waterfall over my head.
Of the human and infant rubble
in Oklahoma City he bemoaned only
what he called the government's
latest scapegoat and considered
what he'd do if agents came
to the door to take his guns —
better to run so they wouldn't kill
his wife and child he guessed.
Should I fear him or what he fears?
He's the one who says he'd
do something about it if he saw
a woman raped — not like those
New Yorkers, dozens staring,
getting off or too scared to act.
Should I fear him or the ones
he fears — eight black guys stopped his cab.
If it weren't for this gun — it was tucked,
then I knew it, under his seat —
I'd be dead now. Should I fear him
or the one he fears, I who believe,
little do-gooder, daydreamer, girlscout
that we should have no guns, no sovereign states,
no infidelity, no greed. I'm the only woman
walking here alone under the crowning trees.
Rich houses on the hill across the street
train their glass eyes on the distant flowering.

POEM FOR MY FATHER TOI DERRICOTTE

You closed the door.
I was on the other side,
screaming.

It was black in your mind.
Blacker than burned-out fire.
Blacker than poison.

Outside everything looked the same.
You looked the same.
You walked in your body like a living man.
But you were not.

would you not speak to me for weeks
would you hang your coat in the closet without saying hello
would you find a shoe out of place and beat me
would you come home late
would i lose the key
would you find my glasses in the garbage
would you put me on your knee
would you read the bible to me in your smoking jacket after
    your mother died
would you come home drunk and snore
would you beat me on the legs
would you carry me up the stairs by my hair so that my feet
    never touch bottom
would you make everything worse
to make everything better

i believe in god, the father almighty,
the maker of heaven, the maker
of heaven and my hell.

would you beat my mother
would you beat her till she cries like a rabbit
would you beat her in a corner of the kitchen
while i am in the bathroom trying to bury my head underwater
would you carry her to the bed
would you put cotton and alcohol on her swollen head
would you make love to her hair

would you caress her hair
would you rub her breasts with ben gay until she stinks
would you sleep in the other room in the bed next to me while
    she sleeps on the pull-out cot
would you come on the sheet while i am sleeping. later i look
    for the spot
would you go to embalming school with the last of my
    mother's money
would i see your picture in the book with all the other
    black boys you were the handsomest
would you make the dead look beautiful
would the men at the elks club
would the rich ladies at funerals
would the ugly drunk winos on the street
know ben
pretty ben
regular ben

would your father leave you when you were three with a mother
    who threw butcher knives at you
would he leave you with her screaming red hair
would he leave you to be smothered by a pillow she put
    over your head
would he send for you during the summer like a rich uncle
would you come in pretty corduroys until you were nine and
    never heard from him again

would you hate him
would you hate him every time you dragged hundred pound
    cartons of soap down the stairs into white ladies'
    basements
would you hate him for fucking the woman who gave birth
    to you
hate him flying by her house in the red truck
    so that the other father threw down his hat in the street
    and stomped on it angry like we never saw him
(bye bye
to the will of grandpa
bye bye to the family fortune
bye bye when we stomped that hat,
to the gold watch,
embalmer's palace,
grandbaby's college)

mother crying silently, making floating island
sending it up to the old man's ulcer

would grandmother's diamonds
close their heartsparks
in the corner of the closet
like the yellow eyes of cockroaches?

Old man whose sperm swims in my veins,

come back in love, come back in pain.

FEARS OF THE EIGHTH GRADE TOI DERRICOTTE

When I ask what things they fear,
their arms raise like soldiers volunteering for battle:
Fear of going into a dark room, my murderer is waiting.
Fear of taking a shower, someone will stab me.
Fear of being kidnapped, raped.
Fear of dying in war.
When I ask how many fear this,
all the children raise their hands.

I think of this little box of consecrated land,
the bombs somewhere else,
the dead children in their mothers' arms,
women crying at the gates of the bamboo palace.

How thin the veneer!
The paper towels, napkins, toilet paper — everything
burned up in a day.

These children see the city after Armageddon.
The demons stand visible in the air
between their friends talking.
They see fire in a spring day
the instant before conflagration.
They feel blood through closed faucets,
the dead rising from the boiling seas.

PANTOUM OF THE WORKING CLASSES

SEAN THOMAS DOUGHERTY

Children run through streets of garbage.
They kick against the politicians' pities.
How many will be found in closed garages?
Beneath the factory smoke of dying cities

They kick against the politicians' pities;
Their fathers boozing at the union bars
Beneath the factory smoke of dying cities,
Wasted afternoons huffing gasoline from jars.

Their fathers boozing at the union bars,
A gang of teenagers robs a corner store;
Wasted afternoons huffing gasoline from jars
In an abandoned house with blown out doors.

A gang of teenagers robs a corner store;
They steal a case of beer, a bag of chips.
In an abandoned house with blown out doors,
They laugh about this world of crazy shit.

They steal a case of beer, a bag of chips,
Climb the roof to drink and count the stars;
They laugh about this world of crazy shit;
Their fathers getting drunk at union bars.

Climb the roof to drink and count the stars,
Forget the fear of boredom that they breathe;
Their fathers getting drunk at union bars,
They argue there is nothing to believe:

How many will be found in closed garages?
Our children run through streets of garbage.

CRATER FACE DENISE DUHAMEL

is what we called her. The story was
that her father had thrown Drano at her
which was probably true, given the way she slouched
through fifth grade, afraid of the world, recess
especially. She had acne scars
before she had acne — poxs and dips
and bright red patches.
                              I don't remember
any report in the papers. I don't remember
my father telling me her father had gone to jail.
I never looked close to see the particulars
of Crater Face's scars. She was a blur, a cartoon
melting. Then, when she healed — her face,
a million pebbles set in cement.
                              Even Comet Boy,
who got his name by being so abrasive,
who made fun of everyone, didn't make fun
of her. She walked over the bridge
with the one other white girl who lived
in her neighborhood. Smoke curled
like Slinkies from the factory stacks
above them.
                    I liked to imagine that Crater Face
went straight home, like I did, to watch Shirley Temple
on channel 56. I liked to imagine that she slipped
into the screen, bumping Shirley with her hip
so that the child actress slid out of frame, into the tubes
and wires that made the TV sputter when I turned it on.
Sometimes when I watched, I'd see Crater Face
tap-dancing with tall black men whose eyes
looked shiny, like the whites of hard-boiled eggs.
I'd try to imagine that her block was full
of friendly folk, with a lighthouse or goats
running in the street.
                              It was my way of praying,
my way of un-imagining the Drano pellets
that must have smacked against her
like a round of mini-bullets,
her whole face as vulnerable as a tongue
wrapped in sizzling pizza cheese.
How she'd come home with homework,

the weight of her books bending her into a wilting plant.
How her father called her slut, bitch, big baby, slob.
The hospital where she was forced to say it was an accident.
Her face palpable as something glowing in a Petri dish.
The bandages over her eyes.
                              In black and white,
with all that make-up, Crater Face almost looked pretty
sure her MGM father was coming back soon from the war,
seeing whole zoos in her thin orphanage soup.
She looked happiest when she was filmed
from the back, sprinting into the future,
fading into tiny gray dots on UHF.

FOUR HOURS DENISE DUHAMEL

My sister picks up her daughters at the bus stop
ever since a nine-year-old girl from the neighborhood
was coaxed into a car by a man
telling her he'd hit a kitten down the road.
His story went that the small ball of fur
ran somewhere near the railroad tracks
and he needed an extra pair of eyes to find it.
The girl was smart and had been taught
everything grownups thought she'd have to know
about even the worst of strangers, but she wanted
to be a veterinarian when she grew up.
And the man looked as though he'd been crying.
"He had that child in the car four hours,"
my mother tells me, my mother who would cut off his balls
if she had the chance. She sounds fed up, middle-class,
when she says it, and I want to say "no,"
but I too share her sentiment. My father
thinks the rapist deserves worse, to be shot dead —
no questions asked. My brother-in-law has a gun,
and my sister knows he'd use it if anyone tried to touch
their daughters, my nieces, my parents' grandchildren.
Four hours is longer than some double features,
longer than some continental plane rides,
longer than a whole afternoon in grade school.
Nothing is slower than time when you're nine years old,
nothing is more fragile than trust.
The rapist dropped the girl off at the pizza parlor
where the men who worked there called an ambulance.
Before this, my nieces walked the short distance home
and they protest, wanting to know why they can't anymore.
The after-school rapist hasn't been caught,
but the second and fifth grade rumors aren't terrifying enough.
My sister wonders how to tell her daughters,
who love small animals and only want to help.

GRADUALLY STUART DYBEK

it traces the irregularities of pavement,
fills cracks, floods the gaps
planned for expansion in the heat, eddies
into a sticky ring beneath a pop bottle
before pooling in the gutter
the way the socket of an eye is pooled
until every aspect of the street is soaked
in a stretch of shade noon can't erase,
winedark like a birthmark
the chalked outline of a body can't contain.
It fades as it flowed, gradually,
but in the bleaching summer brightness,
beneath outcries of sparrows,
children, though moving in time to the beat
of the outraged boombox they shoulder,
still drop their voices as they pass
through the shadow, and the ball
trotting beside them refuses to cross
the border of the stain.

STAIN STUART DYBEK

Snow was falling last night when I returned
to my parish church. Snow is what brought me
back. Without it I couldn't have traced
my old bootprints, nor would the blood have been
as easy to follow — trailed as if every few steps
someone staggering home from the dentist,
with a handkerchief pressed to his mouth,
had paused to spit out the taste of metal.
Dulled by cold, bells hammered an hour
out of tune with the times.
It was as if the concussion of chimes,
the daily battering of the Angelus,
had worn away stone: below the steeple,
the neighborhood stood devastated —
windows blown inward, walls barely supported
by graffiti, backyards reduced to plots of graves.
The waifs, winos, and petty hoods
who once were local heroes, were wanted now
for crimes against humanity. And a stain,
soaking through snow as if the wounds
of bodies half-buried in the frozen ground
were leaking through gauze, was visible
in every exhaled breath and in the fog
fuming from sewers and the exhausts of limousines
that idled beneath the blink of bar signs,
their brake lights reflecting across black ice.
The river, rusting before the embers
of bankrupt foundries, was an opened vein.

WHEN THE LEATHER IS A WHIP MARTÍN ESPADA

At night,
with my wife
sitting on the bed,
I turn from her
to unbuckle
my belt
so she won't see
her father
unbuckling
his belt

THE COMMUNITY COLLEGE REVISES ITS CURRICULUM
IN RESPONSE TO CHANGING DEMOGRAPHICS
MARTÍN ESPADA

SPA 100 Conversational Spanish
2 Credits

The course
is especially concerned
with giving police
the ability
to express themselves
tersely
in matters of interest
to them

THE MACK CHARLES PARKER LYNCHING

SYBIL PITTMAN ESTESS

(Poplarville, Mississippi, 1959)

I saw the blood. I was sixteen —
Red puddles on white-marble steps.
On Saturday morning, early
after our late-night April prom.

I was a soprano who sang
several romantic solos
at the dance the night before with
the band. They said he had raped her —

a white woman. They could not take
a chance with random justice, for
they had their daughters and their wives,
their secretaries to protect. . . .

The elected deputy sheriff
laid the jail-key on his desk near
open windows in the courthouse
where the jail was then on the top.

(I had visited there that year —
in Sunday School as a witness.
I was all Baptist in our red-brick
white-filled church on Main Street.)

Then he went with the men, the mob,
in the cell and yelled for no one
to notice or tell. No one did
but the one female witness just

blew her brains out — not much later.
But I already knew — oh yes:
the world wasn't good and that white
wasn't white and black merely black.

In my gray earth, my first love left
me for my best friend that same year
I sang those love songs. He was there
dancing so near — with someone else.

When I saw that blood, though, early
on Saturday after Friday
something happened as it had not
before. Soon I'd be seventeen.

My world was all color, counted
chance. I was white and he was black
and it was Mississippi then:
1959. In high school

I would be a senior next year.
Someday I would leave there. The world
was open but oh so scary.
I saw him hold her close that night

I sang "In My Alice Blue Gown,"
a song from the thirties. What time
was I in, anyway, and what
place must I leave from — to flee far?

BACK IN MY DAY, STEVE FAY

Son, we had violence in high school, too, even a shooting
in the cafeteria a year or two before I went there, and cliques
that were popular, and ones that got shat on, and the race riot
a week or so after King was shot, the Socialite white kids
running out of the school to join in the fist fights for fun
and so they could say they did, and then the forty cops
in the halls for the rest of the school that year, and that one
day some of us, blacks and whites, walking back to the main
building from gym class talking about pretending to get
into a fight right next to the SWAT force's armored car,
because why are those helmeted cops hiding in there anyway
unless they're scared, and wouldn't they piss their pants
if they saw a fight break out, but anyway we didn't do it,
but we had guns trained on us, or they were ready with
them guns all that year, and for the whole year after that
a plain-clothes security force took up the same stations in
all the hallways, and every day in our class of forty-five
hundred (you didn't know we had big schools then, too)
there was a fight somewhere, and some say knifings, and I
got jumped a couple of times and punched, but only went down
the time it was these five guys from another school after
a basketball game 'cause I was about the size I am now, but
my friend Ralph got picked on a lot, even though he was wiry
and could wrestle anybody his size, but since he was a shrimp,
it didn't matter much and these guys would poke him
and threaten, and try to trip him, but they'd only do it once
'cause his protection, his only protection, was being smart,
and reading a lot about explosives, and having a pretty easy
time making anybody think he was about ten times smarter
than you and your whole family put together, and so he'd
tell these guys, no matter what group they was in, that if
they hurt him they'd pay for it good — like they'd sit
on the bus one day and find chemicals burning them through
their pants, or they'd get their lockers blown up by a bomb,
and one guy he convinced he could send a homemade
guided missile across the South 'Burbs to blow up
his garage — and I don't know that Ralph never did some of
those things, but I didn't have to worry 'cause he and I

were friends and the only white boys in the whole school with Afro hair styles, and soon everybody hated Nixon more than each other, and at the pep rally we all donned the school colors and cheered on our team of Black basketball stars with: "Sock a little Purple Power to 'em."

FOR MY DAUGHTER REGINALD GIBBONS

1.

I hear your friends in the street;
the day is as still as this room.
Speaking a nickname will turn
a head or raise an answering arm.

Why did you come in? To watch me
at my silent work? Why does
every image of you, however
hair-raising your narrow escapes,

however sulky your thwarted
afternoons, end in this pose? —
you watching me from the doorway
as I sit at my desk, finding the right phrase.

If you put your small hand to my neck
the touch chills. And even before
I look back at you, you begin
to vanish, the walls seem to come clear

through you, the photos and bookshelves
distracting me from you, myself
a distraction. And if you still
do not exist, it's because you never will.

2. (Alternatives)

. . . in the mudslide;
You died when the shack set on fire —
    two rooms, the polished bones of gray planks —
    collapsed in a glowing heap;
You died at the weaving machine
    slumped against the shiny levers,
    your lungs crinkling with nylon dust;
You died after almost escaping the pack of dogs;
You died in the kitchen with your own father's
    bullet in you, your hands raised;
You died with the gang-joke of old rope
    around your throat in the schoolyard;

You died in the infant ward with your mother's
    drugs soaked through your brain
    and your feet and arms lost on the way here;
You died under the weight of the executed townsmen;
You died with your heart wobbling till it burst,
    and the boys walking away, leaving you in the ditch;
You died . . .

3.
Blood clouds the vision: a shape
flickering through the trees
just out of sight, a sheerness,
vapor-thin, trying to appear.

No, vision clouds because there's
nothing to see: the eye strains
till it blurs with tears: a missing date,
a failed prophecy, a mistake.

This sudden urge to turn up the hill street,
taking the long way past the redbud
and dogwood — faint purple haze against
a cloud of white — was it a voice, your voice?

BATTERY DIANE GLANCY

. . . north of Waco, exit I35 on Loop 340 east,
take Elk Road left 3–4 miles to a water tower

I pass a sign, ATF FBI KNOW HOW TO LIE
spray-painted on the side of a metal shed,
a cottonfield like a salvage yard for angels,
then there's nothing but fields broken into by the sky,
trees squatting to the land,
a trough of weeds leaning in the wind.

A few miles, a fork in the road, a blue tank,
I drive on but turn around
and go back to a man mowing the ditch grass.
He can't hear but I find him willing to turn off his motor.
He says, *turn left at the blue water-tank not tower*
go half a mile.

I drive by a hand-painted sign,
don't stop don't even slow down,
and at a shadow of a tree across the road turn around,
but another car comes and seems to slow and I drive on,
disappointed at my hesitancy to walk in,
but settle for another kind of seeing,
a daunted sideways glance
like the runover of a plane trying to make a fogdrop in a field.

But there is nothing to see,
the sunken desks of land,
a pond, a few shacks, a burned-out schoolbus,
another sign something like a burst of yellow on blue
though I can't be sure,
a woman stands in the yard, her hand on her waist
caught in the barewind of her mind.

I don't know what to say in the fervor of religion,
what words he must have preached when he ran into the stars
like a hubcap scraping a median strip,
the sparks, *wow,* when you know you're being seen
like in one of those gas-station restrooms on the highway,
you know they watch you through some hole.

The grass mower said the woman was probably
the wife of the original founder whom David Koresh ran off,
not sweetly playing his harp as David rushed Saul,
but the impounding voice of God,
Noah build a compound it's going to rain,
or the fiery voice of Nebuchadnezzar, *heat the furnace seven times.*
His followers must have talked behind their backs,
he's playing his harmonica, making it up as he goes.

The mower said they've been here for years,
living at first along a ravine in tents like pigs,
the usual story: *a group of them,*
the mower said, *waiting for the end of the world,*
fire or water. It would be both.

He must have gone crazy from rejection and failure
in the world, he just couldn't fit,
but he could father children,
he could instruct them as he thought God would
and there was the sweetest smell of that cut grass.

He tried out the words he brought back from stars
in their green skirts and electric heads.
He could even hear the sermon of the cosmos
when God stepped out with women,
his myriad of believers, and David was a part.
He could have many wives too.
It seems to be the way with men when they could get away with it,
as many as they want.

All his life he'd been a stem pulled from the apple,
now he'd ride the Milky Way on that trail of black smoke,
that cloud-burst from firetrucks
flashing bright as Texas in the sungorged field.

The angels must have torn up their wings getting here,
an afternoon's burnout from finding the place:
Elk Road, blue water-tower left,
there's a sudden burst imploding,
orange-flaked pieces of gunshot from the sun
and the end of the world in the fiery mouth of God.

MY BROTHER'S ANGER   PATRICIA GOEDICKE

And here they are again, the duffel bags of sadness,
Shouldering their way into the house like a football team.

Mute, muscular, swollen,
Straining at the seams

Their small eyes look up
Waiting for me to open them.

Friends, how can I help you?

I want to pick you up, to cradle you in my arms
But I am too heavy myself.

Can't anyone tie his own shoes?

Speak to me, Trouble,
Tell me how to move.

My brother's anger is a helmet.

My sister's voice is a cracked flute
Talking to itself underwater.

What can I offer but a sieve?

Shoving yesterday in a closet
I make small talk, smile

Rush around trying to hang up coats

But all over the house there are these dull
Enormous sacks of pain.

Stumbling over other people's leftover lumber

I keep trying to embrace them,
Battering my head against weathered flanks . . .

Every day more suicides
Among the living, more hangovers

Among the dead.

I throw myself down on the floor
Right in front of them

But it's no use: these slab-sided sorrows
Have taken up permanent residence

And will not be comforted.

COLUMBINE HIGH SCHOOL/LITTLETON, CO

ALBERT GOLDBARTH

Here, thirteen high school students died,
murdered by two other high school students
— the memorial consists
of fifteen crosses. In this photograph, a woman
rests her head against one upright beam
as if decanting
(*trying* to) everything that's in her brain
— only the wood, only something
inhuman now, could hold what flows from her.
This grief's too vast for us, a color of its own,
not from our limited strip of the spectrum.
Really all that makes this picture comprehensible
to us — to we who view, but haven't
lived, this news — is the take-out cup
for her cola. You know, with the plastic lid
and the straw. A summer movie
advertised around it. Droplets
on the side, from where its ice and the heat
of the afternoon commune.
It's a large. You've had it
on maybe a thousand occasions. Any of us
might hold this drink,
might take it into our systems.

PRAYER TO THE BOYS OF SAN ANTONIO RAY GONZALEZ

The day has no blood to give you.
You give the night its power,

douse street lamps in the night
that unleashes love and laughter,

thriving beat of danger without forgiveness,
hatred for the life you never had as a child.

May the drive-by shatter the philosophers of poverty.
May they find broken glass and never learn hand signals

as you watch them set curfews on television.
May you ignore the world with a fresh round

in the chamber as you protest your
dying brother with blind retaliation.

The city has nothing to give you.
You give the streets power by shooting each other

as if things would change and you could die
for one cause, one color, one street

flaming in the barrio where a passing car
is a torch flying toward the loud ceremony,

bullet-riddled vehicles crashing closer
to the dark offices of the administration,

farther from one neighborhood where day-glow
letters spell a language for one city.

JOSÉ'S JAPANESE SWORD RAY GONZALEZ

He cut the officer's head off,
kept the weapon he wrestled out of his hands.
I saw the dent in the blade
when I was a boy,
Samurai sword hanging on the wall.

He showed it to me after thirty years,
my uncle's delight over a life of war
brittle and honorable,
the blade speechless in his hands,

the museum of family secrets a flash
of brilliant light in our jungle,
swish of the blade re-entering the scabbard,
closing the conversation for another generation.

RAPIST: A ROMANCE RIGOBERTO GONZÁLEZ

The quarter shined on his palm like light entering a hole in the bone. If fear had color his hand would have bruised. I wanted to place the tip of my nipple on the icy metal just to understand him a little more. Instead I took the coin and watched his body float backwards as if I had lifted its last anchor. He waved good-bye. The last speech in his mouth spilled out the way I had made him give up his words many times: thickly and slowly and red.

Our first night together I watched him sleep so peacefully I could have slit his throat. I held the tip of the knife inside his nostril, his ear, his navel; he might have itched in his dream. I let him live through the night and I knew he would leave me some day. The next morning I kissed his eyes through the lenses of his glasses. I disappeared behind the smudges. It was useless to see me coming.

I call him Pretty Cock because it was so perfect when it stiffened into carved stone. The skin of its head matched the nipples matched the anus and I realized what a simple confection he was. I confirmed it by what small imagination he displayed when he left and came back to me, wearing the same socks, speaking the same basic vocabulary of *love* and *yes* and *no* and *please*.

He was irresistible in that white terry cloth robe that curtained the hairy hamstrings of his legs as he bent over to check the bath. He was irresistible in the wet sleeve letting go of its clear coins on the black bathroom tile. He was irresistible slumped across the bathtub with the dark algae of his hair opening and closing on the surface of the water. Fucking him while he almost drowned — that was irresistible.

He told me how when he was twelve his mother had killed herself while he watched from the door as she took pill after pill as if in a trance. I told him how when I was fourteen my father had watched me do sit-ups in the living room until the night he pulled my legs over his shoulders and made me shit on his cock. He told me he had tried to kill himself the same way his mother had. I told him I didn't have a choice either.

Amor, I miss pressing my tongue to your pulse as I clench your wrist between my teeth. I miss the discovery of your heartbeat as I bite your neck. You said we fucked like cats and that night you clawed your way out from under me and made me chase you to the balcony. I pressed against you on the railing. I miss your back magnet-sticky on my chest like that. I could have pierced you perfectly so that your head slid painlessly through the moon's silver ring. But I missed.

I saw him waiting for the bus one afternoon. The black coat made him look like a piece of iron balanced on the curb. I wanted to push it forward to flatten on the street with the heavy clang of metal vibrating through every vein of concrete. But I wasn't letting go that easily. Not yet. Not with that quarter still burning a hole in my stomach since the last time he left. He said to call him once I got over my fist-to-jaw reflex and I swallowed the coin just to spite him.

ADVICE TO A COMING CHILD

BENJAMIN SCOTT GROSSBERG

Don't complain too much. Your father
played my father, briefly, and he doesn't
like screaming or shouting,
and doesn't know how to deal with crying.

Be very thankful. For everything.
Your father will give you gifts
and responsibilities as if they are gifts,
and will misunderstand a gesture

if it's not right. You'll find it easy
to be branded in that household, so learn
stealth early. Child, learn how to seem,
find the looks and words that stop

your father's heart cold. It won't
be easy for you in that house;
it's strange to know that now, to know
how much you will love your father

though he won't be by most standards
good to you, to know how little
he'll acknowledge your love,
to know about the violence

throughout your childhood,
and the terrible years afterwards
when you discover what you father was
and how little any of it had to do

with you. I will be old by then, child,
and detached from you and your life.
I will never meet you under your father's roof.
But if my name, which will not

be mentioned in your house
happens to be mentioned just once,
and if you are curious, and have
no brother or sister with whom

to parse out the battery, with whom
to understand the shame, then, child,
you come to me. Old as I am,
wounded or healed, we'll sit

and ponder the animal coming and going,
we'll drink something warm and sweet
and raise a toast, perhaps,
to the joy of coming through.

HOMING IN LILACE MELLIN GUIGNARD

Not hiding behind a ski mask, the man
approaches the teller and demands a withdrawal —

no particular account. Because the gun is frightening
(poking at her from his navy suitcoat, small telescope

bringing the impossible closer) she gives him a full sack,
saying later *he didn't look so crazy*, and he takes it

wishing they could have met in a park or an elevator.
"Thank you," he says thinking *beautiful*. *Polite* she thinks

saying nothing. The police come and leave with the videotape,
except for the rookie who must write the reports. He's in back

when the thief shows up, unarmed, to make a deposit
and of course the teller recognizes him — which is what he wanted.

Wanted it more than he feared a snickering jury
or grown men winking through bars black as the gates on cemeteries

and private schoolyards. This time she hits the silent alarm.
Habit easily overcomes attraction, safety wins over everything,

rock, scissors, paper. . . She's worked that window seven years;
two flubs like this in one day — she'd be fired. What makes

the homing pigeon so predictable? Something buried
far away in a place they'll never reach

gives them enough to steer by. And people enjoy returning
to what they know, the café for coffee every morning

where the man at the register says "Hello" followed by your name
and the waitress knows you take cream and Sweet 'N Low.

The places where, through repetition, we insist we belong
help us believe in continuation, relieve the terror

of bulldozed grade school haunts or lover's doors now locked.
When does our quest for comfort become madness?

There are places where none of us can remember having been
yet would return to if given the chance, would risk it all

to sit snug and safe, moving back and forth in one spot
the way prisoners and lunatics do in films, the way our mothers

rocked us in the asylum of their bellies.

The parking lots of K-Mart are not safe. There are video cameras on school buses, and metal detectors in the halls of universities. Every time she gives an F she feels something burn into the back of her neck.

When the telephone rings again at three A.M. with breathing, and you startle awake, you know the police can do nothing, unless afterwards. The chain rattling at your entry cannot kill you. So you tell yourself, as you dial 911, the believer's number.

Elsewhere, food sent to starving Somalis is sold in little heaps on the street: rice, flour, the dry powder that is milk. In Bosnia, children are born already raped. Their mothers do not know any more what to love.

There is a man held in the dark. He is not allowed to speak. One day, the chatter of the guards, record played backwards, fades out. At the man's door a poem softly knocks. He memorizes it. The poem is his charm, his small control. It is how he stays alive.

JACKED LOLA HASKINS

You tap on my window with a gun.
You want my car. It's yours

you gesture. Slide over.
I thought you wanted my car.

The day's as clear as a windshield.
The road's as hard as this thing

in my throat that won't let go.
You squeal a left. The street

turns dirt. You stop. Rope
uncurls like a snake from

your pocket. *Get out*, you say.
Lie down. One foot on my spine,

you tug the rope. Ants swarm
up my legs. Fine sand

grits my cheek. You drive away.
Night after night, like illness,

like bad fish stuffed in my mouth,
I bring you back.

TEN STILL LIVES JUAN FELIPE HERRERA

Man flying over bridge with orange sunset on shirt
Chain-walk through the mainline with ragged cuffs against red ankles
President at banquet with sheep in background
Mayor naked on purplish pillow with cocaine dish
Maid in master's kitchen with fast butcher knife
Ditch diggers on Broadway with three-piece suit sociologists
Girl in morgue freezer with boyfriend's blue ribbon on neck
48 stitches over thorax with two mortadella torpedos on the side
Husband in cheap hotel with mini-truck smoking
Two breasts touching with two breasts touching

THE BOND BOB HICOK

He gets
robbed, a knife in his chest and two
doctors holding his arms and two
his legs and one pumping blood from his lung
and a scream as constant as the speed
of light because he's not anesthetized
and why oh why the god-damned cigarettes
at 2 A.M.? He heals quickly because
he stops smoking and converts to a low-
sodium diet and learns to meditate
on a window-seat with a view of the bay
until his wrists and lips tingle
with the low-voltage love of inner peace.
Life goes back to bananas and dusting
and wanting to ask strangers the history
of their tattoos and looking
for God among the wounded architecture
of factories. Life returns to dreams
of Dolores Del Rio and trying to hold
someone's eyes on the subway long enough
to feel that a discourse of souls
is still possible. The scar entertains
his fingers, is kissed by the woman he loves
as birds must adore the sky, grows so deep
into memory that his body would be broken
without it. For two years he calls
the cop with a voice like Walter Cronkite
and says *anything* with a rising inflection
and the cop says *nothing* like it's the sound
of every breath he takes and hangs up
very softly to apologize. For two years
he pretends he doesn't flinch
at the brown faces and beautiful names
of boys and men who pass on the street
in reds and greens and blues
that could be the colors of a gang
or just light fulfilling its desire to be
everything at once. Then the cop comes by
and says he thinks they got the guy
and the guy's got a hole and the hole's
the last thing he touched. The cop

stops by and ask if he'll come down
and look at the body and he says of course.
And he does go down and look at the body
and it is the guy only he says it's not,
only he says he can't remember
these eyes or hands, only he trembles
at the disclosure of the hole and says
he can't recall anything even though
he's carried this face around and beaten
this body and pissed in this mouth every night
for two years of revenge less tangible than wind.
He gets
out, goes home to his rug and plants
and walls that breathe every hundred
years and a view of the bay where water
migrates with constant adoration. He comes
home and strips and lies on the floor
and touches the scar so long that the sound
of cars and feel of his breath and image
of the man on a silver table fuse like glass
rolling red from the furnace. Then it's dusk
and his lover's touching his body like braille
and asking how his day went, hands and tongue
weightless as ash. Then it's dusk and he hears
a voice saying *fine, ok, good*, feels hands
on his shoulders and a tongue circling
his nipples, crossing back and forth
over the scar as if erasing, licking back
and forth as if wounds are what we most
dearly love.

MONIQUE CYNTHIA HOGUE

I feel raped by being robbed until
my student's raped. The man, a father
from the daycare center where she works,
stopped by to "talk about his son."

Surprised alone, she let him in.
Her cop boyfriend did not want the guys
at work to know. It took her two days
to file a report, against his will.

The rapist, who had a record,
skipped state. I make the calls
she needs — hotline, counselor, doctor
(HIV tests must wait) — and offer

what I have: a safe place, this ugly
office with its split-pea walls and dead,
ant-eaten palmetto bugs I cannot bear
to touch. She comes to last class,

turns in her study of the Barbie doll.
It's full of carefully-collaged pictures,
poetry. She says she's *all right,*
she'll move to Tampa this summer

with her boyfriend who really
understands now. When she leaves,
I leaf through her dream-life
which I cannot grade or keep.

1.
"He reminds me of a man who once sold me a green tuxedo."

2. *Family Values*
The years-long feud between brothers. The incest.
Wife-beating when drunk, or whenever.
They dumped her in a home.
Humiliations. *(You _____ !)* Child
molestation. *Nobody's business.* If you didn't flaunt it,
adultery. *Everyone does it.* Faithlessness.
I'm cutting you out of the will.
The local priest, the daycare worker, names
in the paper. *He had his reasons.*
She asked for it.
Dirty linen, they said. The father who left.
The father they never met. *They'll get over it.*
The boy will. Disowning the gay son.
The girl will get married someday, she'll have kids of her own —
What will the neighbors think. The smile forced on.

3.
You thought there was somebody there, but then when you looked,
    they were gone.
Not even a leaf moving.

4. *From Interviews (St. Paul, 1991)*
It was a pretty small cross.
It wasn't like he shot anybody. Nothing else
caught on fire. It was an expression
of free speech. Are you saying
I don't have rights? I don't, and they do? Maybe
he shouldn't have put it on their lawn. OK, so maybe
next time put it on public land. In the town square.
In front of the jail. In front of the courthouse.
It was only a prank. You know? It was only a joke.
Another thing about them: they can't take a joke.

5. *The Green Tuxedo*
It's Amos 'n Andy, the old TV show. They're sitting on a porch, and a
beautiful fancy car pulls up and parks. A handsome man gets out, and
a beautiful fancy woman with a big, elegant dog on a leash — perhaps

a Russian wolfhound — gets out, and they walk slowly past Amos 'n
Andy. Amos turns to Andy (or was it the other way round?) and says,
"He reminds me of a man who

6.

Meaning, *he sold me something I didn't need?*
Something nobody needs?
Something beautiful but useless?
Something I only wore once?
Something that impressed my lover?
that made me look ridiculous?
that quickly went out of style?
that I never looked at again?
that I buried in the closet?
that I secretly loved?
that shamed me?

7. World Affairs

The woman with a son in the Gulf wears his picture
as a button on her jacket. She is accorded some status,
as were women required to breed for the state in Romania.
She hates every boy his age who is not there. She loves
the President. In the video-game war nobody dies.
The soldiers worry that one of them may be gay,
may be watching in the shower —
    and what do the young men in Bosnia fear,
     who every day work in the rape camps?
In the video-game war only nobodies died.
The woman with a son in the Gulf knows
who the enemy is.

8.

turns to him and says, "He reminds me of a man who

9.

Meaning, *he's a questionable character?*
He'll take advantage of me?
I don't know what he's up to?
He has something I want?
I don't trust him?
I don't like him?
I'm afraid of him?
I hate him?

10.

Not even a leaf moving. Check the back seat:
it's empty. You get in. Driving the right roads: busy,
but not congested. Driving not too fast, not
too slowly. All the doors locked.
It's the end of the century.
You just want to get home.

NIGHT OF THE HUNTER PAUL HOOVER

According to the theory,
Madonna erased Madonna Ciccone;
white men erased the Cherokee nation;
Serbs erased Muslims; black men erase
black men; and guns erase everyone else
as night erases day.
    Everything is erased
including the trace of history,
which, like a cartoon dog,
draws the trail with his nose
but erases it with his tail.
Half erasure, half wisdom,
history rocks in her chair like Lillian Gish
in *Night of the Hunter*, a shotgun
in her lap. She loves the black-frocked
stranger with LOVE and HATE
tattooed on his fingers, despite
his being white and crazy — the kind of person
children flee like insects from a fire.
After locking him in the barn,
history waits for the sheriff's siren
to wail out of some perfect future
where everything is revealed, everything forgiven.
As poetry thrives on a perfect indifference,
history grows from hate and love.
It's like taking a nature walk
in the outer blast zone, where,
hidden in his burrow, a single badger
drags to the surface the accidental seeds
that will reconstruct the green forest.
This leads to other life and later of course
murder. The fox must have its mouse;
the mouse has lice. I read the other day
that some of the early Germans inhabiting
this country were so pacifistic
they refused to raise a hand when
the Delaware warriors killed their wives
and children. It was god's will,
they said: *One must never kill*.
One of them, however, kept a loaded gun,
and when a Delaware tribesman

walked over a rise, he shot him
in the forehead. The pacifists banished
him forever, and that is history.
We do the best we can to keep
from being erased. But time and the moment
wear us down. We are here and gone,
a flicker on the screen brilliantly remembered.
Even as we speak, words change the shape
of our mouths, creating and erasing
the captions beneath our faces:
(1) most authentic (2) hurricane victim
(3) future engineer (4) politically correct.
Pure form is finally shapeless,
or words to that effect. In an age of private jargon,
one can always make the dead zebra stand.
At century's dead end or walking
into stars, what was done to us
was done with our consent and shines more fiercely
than we are allowed to remember.
In the entry to that place, a beaded purse
from Oklahoma is ripped from fragile hands.

PANIC AUSTIN HUMMELL

In the night woods, any stir is sudden —
a syrinx fallen to leaves, the shuffle
of a goat's foot, the sound of your own voice

startling the silence a capella.
Even kids own the awe of a god there,
ruminant in cover, redolent of sweat.

So we named a new fear in the forest,
half for a wanton god, half for the sightless
alarm it caused us, flaming like contagion.

Some terror we never get used to —
like the tales of children lost to the Black
Forest, the pruning of a daughter's limbs,

the grim click of switches and closing doors.
We try to forget — when halfway through life
the swirl of blue lights and sirens shocks us

to the icy shoulder of an alien road,
when the plane we're in dips and pivots
in a pocket of wind, when the phone at 3 A.M.

flushes sweat into the cradle of our palm —
that the woods are still alive, deserted

by parents, that no forest is as dark
as the violence we wake to, children still.

UNHOLY SONNET MARK JARMAN

He loads his weapons, but the Lord God sees him.
He hears the inner voice that tells him, "Yes,"
The voice that tells him, "No." And the Lord sees him,
Watching as he listens first to one voice,
A melody, then the other, like a latch
That slips and catches, slips, until it clicks.
The Lord God sees the hard decision taken,
Watching with his seven compound eyes,
As intimate as starlight, as detached.
He sees between the victims and the killer
Each angle of trajectory. Unshaken,
He sees the horror dreamed and brought to being
And still maintains his vigil and his power,
Which you and I would squander with a scream.

UNHOLY SONNET MARK JARMAN

This boy listening eagerly to his friend
Who wears a steel-studded leather wristband
And catechizes him in petty theft
(The kind that leaves a shop clerk dead for pennies) —
This boy, if you could grab him by the wrist
And contradict his thug worship with visions,
As real as TV, of his life in prison,
Might transfer his attention unto you.
But what about his friend? Too late for him?
Before he enters the quick stop and reveals
The weapon he will use to beat or kill
The man or woman breathing behind the counter,
He pulls a nylon stocking over his head.
Look for the sacred face inside that face.

PINK TRIANGLES LARRY WAYNE JOHNS

After midnight. Drunk.
Too young for the clubs,
I was hanging near the entrance
to Piedmont Park. A silhouette
stepped out of the shadows,
bummed a smoke, asked me to follow
into the woods. I ignored him
as a group of kids, my age,
came strolling down the street.
The man was whispering
Come on, let's go.
He started to ease back
the way one might
back away from a growling dog.
I heard it before I saw it
dangling from one boy's hand —
the aluminum baseball bat
scraping pavement.

Now, whenever I step
over a pink triangle
along the sidewalk in Midtown,
a number inside it tells me
how many of us have been slain.
And I think of that man, that night,
the way I ran for my own life.
I think it's time to stop running.

TATTOO PETER JOHNSON

There's a tattoo of a tiny gun on my hand symbolic of the tiny wars I wage inside myself. Its barrel beckons like the phallus that's visible when you stare directly at the sun. My father said, "A man who can't fight is disgusting." He was half-right about that. Most fathers are, even the one who erected a basketball backboard outside my bedroom window. In the evening, when the sun shrugs its tense shoulders, neighborhood children are rewarded with ice cream. But I'm sent to bed, where I stare at the tiny doorknob tattooed on my other hand until I fall asleep.

ACCOMPLICE PETER JOHNSON

Suicide letters from strangers, stained pages stinking of fear. He saves them, staples them to walls, stores boxes of them in the attic. Sometimes he opens a desk drawer and listens to their panicky conversations, or at night he hears them whisper inside his mattress.

Hard to keep a sense of humor with so many letters. Right now, he imagines the glazed eyes of a black mail truck slicing through snowy side streets down the muddy road to his house. He hears canvas bags, too heavy to carry, dragged across the front porch, letters dropped through a mail slot.

He needs to know why he receives these letters, why the half-dead send woes to him, complete with details of clumsy suicides, of instruments they use. He needs to know what kind of service he's offering, who employs him, why he's still under lock and key.

ON VIEWING TWO DIFFERENT DATE RAPE MOVIES

ALLISON JOSEPH

Both movies star actresses better known
for playing daughters on sitcoms,
faces familiar as students you once had,
or girls you knew yourself in college.
Each movie begins with a raucous frat party
filled with beer-guzzling white boys
(though each frat has its token non-white)
who ambush young women because
they're there, which must mean they want it,
they're asking for it. In both movies
the former sitcom daughters drink
far more than they can handle
then stumble into a room to escape
the swilling throngs, passing out
only to find their boyfriend's best friend
or their older brother's best friend
on top, thrusting in. But here's where
the movies part — the made for tv one
starring that round-faced girl from "Full House"
is so violent you can't mistake this act
for anything else — he rips her clothes,
ignores her screams, thrusts so hard
she can't move, and when he's done,
she runs off crying, trying to cover herself,
blouse torn. In the theatrical movie,
the redheaded daughter from "Kate and Allie"
lies there stunned, passed out,
makeshift toga baring stark skin.
When he mounts her, her cries are faint,
tired, but she doesn't fight, protest mumbled
until he's all the way inside, and her face
reveals just where he's invaded, how far.
All the while he coos about her beauty.
Which is the version to believe?
Which actress is more wounded,
more authentic? Which one looks
like a favorite niece or your best student
from two semesters ago
who sat weeping in your office

for no reason she would name?
When do these stop being movies
and start being something you catch
on their faces, shoulders, checking
for scratches when you're taking roll,
hoping each Monday learning can happen
after the weekend, the parties,
the encounters you're never privy to?

LIGHTER FLUID RODGER KAMENETZ

Until I could remember that I set her on fire
I would suffer, though it was obvious only I
could have set her on fire, while she was sleeping.
There was a thought of lighter fluid in the cabinet
I could see the can with the rusted bottom
felt the cool metal and hefted it for a moment
but could I have been the one to sprinkle her body
while she slept, and lit the match, and watched
the flames rise in the skirts of fumes?

All I remember was seeing her lying there
with the flames rising from her body in yellow tongues
and smothering them with a blanket
for I could not let her burn.
And was I the culprit? There was no one else
on the scene, who could have done it,
that was what their eyes said,
though no one said a thing.

But until I could perforate — that was the technical term
they used — perforate what? — the memory, let it
burst through, remember the moment when I took the can
from the shelf and sprinkled it on her as she lay sleeping
on her back, until I could perforate the memory
I was in an agony of knowing and not knowing
guilty by circumstance, but not yet entered
into the walls of conscience, standing outside
while everyone accused me with their eyes
knowing and not knowing that I had burned her —
who would not sleep with me that night
could I blame her? — from now on my life
was broken like an egg, and nothing could glue it
back together, for the delicate shell was shattered
and the yolk was streaming through — except

I could not perforate, could not break through
to the moment — a skin had grown around it —
or was I fooling myself out of guilt?
Had I really done it? Could I be blaming myself
for something I hadn't done? How could I have set her
on fire while she lay sleeping, dreaming there?

Cock-
ed and forever loaded. Bonecrusher, meatgrinder, brain-
    splatterer.
Weapon of individual destruction. Hitler's rock-hard
    brush.
Widow maker spreads
Everywhere: ghetto, schoolyard,
Workplace. Dead
Flowers hang from
Its snout. Whore of
Metal, powder, pin.

HALF-DEAD DAVID KIRBY

We invite maybe five or six authors here every spring
    for our writers' festival
and book most of them into the downtown Hilton,
    it being reasonably priced
and centrally located, although it is hard for me to go there
    to pick up a poet or drop off
a novelist without thinking of the night I was walking by
    about eleven and heard this moaning

from the shadows and went over to take a look and found
    this poor unhappy miserable woman
who had tried to kill herself by jumping off the top
    of the parking deck, which is maybe
forty feet from the ground and therefore not high enough to be
    lethal. She had compound leg fractures,
though, and I could see these bones sticking through
    the cloth of her trousers. . . .

For a moment I just panicked and sort of stuttered
    and waved my hands in the air,
but then I said to myself, All right, David,
    let's get organized here,
and I bent over her and said, Can you hear me?
    but the woman just went, Uh, uh,
so I took off my jacket and made a pillow and put it under her head,
    and suddenly she sucked in her breath

and grabbed my arm and said, Don't you dare
    get any blood on my blouse,
and I said, Why, you, you ungrateful, you,
    which is when I caught myself
and thought, okay, no need to add insult to injury here.
    Besides, she had let me go
and was going, Uh, uh again, so I said, I'm going for help
    and ran out into the street

where, as luck would have it, the first passerby was
    a sheriff's deputy on a motorcycle,
and I flagged him down and said, Come here, come here,
    there's this injured woman,
and he eased the strap on his holster, and I said,

Look, I didn't do it,
she jumped off the top of the parking deck, and the deputy
    put his head back and squinted

and took a good long look at the deck while I ran back
    to where the woman was,
and by now she had gotten up off my jacket and was trying
    to crawl off down the sidewalk,
so I said, Look, you're going to have to lie still
    or else you're going to hurt yourself,
which may sound paradoxical out of context,
    but the way I figured it,

suicide is probably an all-or-nothing proposition,
    and that someone who has botched
the job is just as interested in getting well as you and I are
    when we have a backache
or the flu, even if all they want is to recover as quickly
    as possible so that they can
go ahead and end it all, and I'm half thinking thoughts
    like these and half trying

to get the woman to slow down and quit dragging herself
    down the sidewalk
and at the same time I'm saying, See, there's this deputy here,
    he's going to help you, too,
and, sure enough, the deputy has concluded his scrutiny
    of the Hilton parking deck
and is squatting down cowboy-style and taking
    a good long look at the woman,

only she's in such bad shape that he's saying,
    Oh my god and other things
that don't sound terribly professional, but at least the woman
    has stopped her mad clawing
at the sidewalk and, in fact, has gone completely silent,
    though whether this is because
she has taken my well-meant advice and decided
    to conserve the little life force

that remains to her or has simply passed out
    from the pain, I cannot say,

though at the moment I am betting on the pain,
  because crouching there beside her,
I feel as though someone has pulled back the skin
  of my own legs and is scraping
my bones with the edge of a dull knife,
  and it is everything I can do

to even look at the poor woman, much less
  attempt to soothe her
with what scant comfort I muster, which by now consists of
  There, there, and Shhhhhhh
and words like that, which are punctuated by a tapping sound
  so faint that I don't connect it
with the scene before me even though it goes on and on, tap tap tap,
  and I'm saying, Easy, easy

and Gently now, tap tap, and finally I look around,
  and it's the damned deputy:
he's sitting with his legs stretched out in a big vee
  and has fainted and keeps
falling forward and then waking up and looking at the woman
  with the broken legs and passing out again,
and the tapping noise is his helmeted head
  hitting the sidewalk.

So now I have a woman with compound fractures
  and a deputy with the vapors,
and I'm thinking, Shit. . . . And the worst part is that
  there is absolutely nobody else
on what is normally a street crowded with shoppers,
  business people, and partygoers,
but tonight for some reason it's a cemetery,
  and it looks as though

there might be a fresh grave any minute here,
  maybe two. I go over
to the deputy's motorcycle and start to screw around
  with his radio so I can "radio for help"
they way they do in the movies: an engine conks out,
  the plane starts to go down,
and somebody yells, Radio for help! as though everyone
  would know exactly what to do.

But I can't find the right buttons
    and succeed only
in generating a high-pitched shriek which makes me
    jump back and clap my hands
over my ears and the suicide woman howl in protest
    and the deputy sit up straight
and look around big-eyed for a second and then nose-dive
    for the sidewalk again, tap, tap, tap.

Now I used to have this German professor who,
    when we came to something difficult
or time-consuming or incomprehensible, would say,
    "*Überspringen wir das,*"
which always struck me as vividly pictorial:
    I'd see the class in their lederhosen
walking down a nice smooth path paved with nouns and verbs
    and articles and adjectives,

and suddenly we'd come across the ablative
    or the pluperfect conditional
jutting up like a big jagged boulder, and, whoosh,
    we'd *überspringen* the whole thing
and land safely on the other side. I wish we could
    do that all the time;
unfortunately, life is more demanding than German.
    Also, when a couple finally appeared,

here is what they saw: a badly injured woman
    on the sidewalk, a deputy sheriff
with his head between his knees, and me standing beside
    the deputy's motorcycle with my hands
over my ears. They ran off in the opposite direction,
    but they must have made a call,
because within minutes a police car and an ambulance arrived,
    so I gave my statement and left.

A few days later I phoned the sheriff's department to see
    what had happened to the woman,
but the person I talked to was very sarcastic, and it made me think
    that a lot of people
who are involved with crimes phone in pretending to be helpful
    or sympathetic when what

they really want is to get information they're not supposed to have
    so they can go out

and create more mayhem. So after a few Yeeahs
    and some Suuurres
and even a Now wouldn't you like to know,
    I decided to skip
the whole thing and said, Thanks, you've been very helpful,
    because who wants to get on
the bad side of the sheriff's department? I still haven't found out
    what happened to the woman,

but if you think of all the things you've learned
    when you weren't trying
to learn them, you'll understand why I think I still might
    find out that she died or recovered
and straightened up or recovered and killed herself
    or some other permutation,
because it's not exactly as though there's this narrative that we plug into
    every time the alarm clock goes off;

it's more as though there's this internal narrative
    just under the surface
which, sooner or later, creates patterns, so that you end up with
    a half-dead woman, a fainting deputy,
and an incompetent rescuer, all in the same physical plane.
    And there's your story.
But the same story could have gone a hundred different ways,
    so maybe it's still going.

Between pillage and rape this relief:

> *My young brother asked me what happens*
> *after we die. I told him we get buried*
> *under a bunch of dirt — then worms eat our*
> *bodies. I guess I should have told him*
> *the truth — that most of us go to hell and*
> *burn eternally. But I didn't want to*
> *upset him.*

Mercy is what happens, isn't it, when one
shows mercy. Well, here at home
things go swimmingly. Across the street
twins the size of barsoap appear healthy
as little horses. And for the first time
my wife is about to sit them. On the phone
she told their mother, I know what to do
if only you tell me how to do it.

If that's news to me, it's old news.
When she leaves I'll pour myself
another cup of coffee
and finish the paper. Until then
mayhem will just have to wait:
    sniper with a schoolgirl in the crosshairs,
    arsonist with his thumbnail at the head
       of a kitchen match,
    terrorist with a stick of high explosive
       up his kamikaze sleeve.

Mostly it's a matter of religion or politics or sex,
or all three, that sometimes holy, sometimes
otherwise trinity, or the claim that something,
for reasons beyond human explanation,
snapped. Your Honor: Pop goes the weasel.

The twins, believe me, are beautifully addictive.
I had left the sniper, arsonist, terrorist
lying on the beige rug beside the green couch
to cross the street

to kichy-coo them. One girl, one boy. Two
miracles, two explanations
of that which cannot be explained, least of all
by the recurring news that Carmen Somewhere
South of the Border has seen, again,
the face of Christ on a tortilla.

At the end of *Gentleman Jim Corbett*
Errol Flynn says, I'm no gentleman, and
Alexis Smith responds: And I'm no lady.

Such honesty, in my book — at times modified
by mercy — deserves praise while
constituting news. So I speak to the twins
as if I expect them to understand. When grin
turns to fuss I assure them that mother, full-
breasted, their Dairy Queen, as their grandmother
calls her, will be home anon. In their innocence,
or in spite of it, neither
seems to believe me. They fuss on.

I too told my younger brother awful things
that might not have been true
to console him. I'm no gentleman, he said
half a lifetime later, and such honesty, in my
book, redeems him.

Blue pj's for the boy, pink for the girl, and full-
breasted the Dairy Queen returns, and together
my wife and I succumb to the moment. Adios and
golly and goodbye. We cross the street
to enter the house
where sniper and arsonist and terrorist
lie near the couch
disarmingly one-dimensional.

Who knows what evil lurks in the hearts of men?
I sat by the radio, wanting an answer,
my brother not far away, peeling an orange. The
Shadow, of course, knows, but
what does it mean to be The Shadow? And what
does it know? In and out I go

with what goes in and out with me. For
there is nothing new under the sun, I'm told,
including the sun, and tomorrow, says Scarlett,
her name no less than her tongue the color almost
of eternal fire, is another day.

THE WRECKAGE ALONG THE RIVER JEFF KNORR

The green truck,
at night on the Sproul Road
is where it all came apart.
He was shot along the river.

He tells it now, as we sit
end to end on this moth-eaten couch,
like it was just a week ago.
I can't imagine the pain
when the bullet slammed
into his neck, snapping
the collar bone at the base
and careening out the right side.
He says he just don't remember.

But that's the small of it,
like a residue of dirt after long work.
Tell me how much it must hurt
to have to build fence with a bum arm,
to have two beautiful boys
by two beautiful women,
neither around anymore.
Tell me about a war
that makes a friend
shoot a friend one dark night
in the wind along a lonely
curve in the river.

In the turning light of dusk
hurt floats in the hungry sky.
And like the report of the deer rifle
one drunk night, this pain
echoes through canyons for miles,
and comes to rest on slow, churning currents.

WARSCAPE, WITH LOVERS MARILYN KRYSL

Scent of plumeria, and the smell of burning.
Not one or the other, but both. Destruction, and the blossom.
Sweetheart, I'm afraid. That boy with the rifle breaks
the catechism in two. And in two. Let me
see us whole, beside the sea. My body
busy, paying attention to yours. Already

we rock each other with our voices. Already
we're braiding the invisible cord. That burning
hut on T.V. isn't ours, but could be. My body
could be hers, child at dead breast. That blossom
of blood and bone could be your face. Let me
say truth: no place, no one, is safe. The breaking

of vows, we know, is a given. Sweetheart, you'll break
my heart. I've broken yours, but look: already
you love me again. Destruction and the blossom: let me
say it another way: that soldier, burning
to become fabulous, torches the thatch (see blossomy
flame) of the enemy's hospital: cut to my body.

MY GUN HAS SO MANY PLACES TO HIDE DAVID LAZAR

Sometimes under my arm where I keep it warm.

Sometimes, after I shoot it, in a metal box that is cool to the touch.

Under the pillow, so I can keep it safe while it sleeps.

In a place close to you, though you never know.

Sometimes in a very public place, where women and shadows do a
slow, strange dance.

A very pretty piece of satin that looks like it's lit from within.

In my heart when the bullets need to burst out of my skin.

Under a tissue on my lap when it is sad and the barrel sheds tears like a
sacred relic.

Near a public telephone that is always ringing, like my left ear.

Sometimes at the home of a friend I have known since I was a grown
man.

At Roseland, where it gets a little drunk and wants to come out and
circle the room.

In a graveyard where a little boy has just been buried who also had a
gun that liked to hide.

In the snow, but only when it falls and only when it isn't white.

Sometimes in a shadow that takes my shape.

Under a floor-board and you never know when it will groan.

Under a small medal of St. Christopher that the nun said was mine to
keep for always.

ETHER LAURENCE LIEBERMAN

Choke-and-Rob, it's   *a Choke-and-Rob nation. If you must*
go on the streets,   *dress only in rags and feathers . . .*
Guyana sneakthieves   *go to school* to the gutter rats, who

blow on the eyelids   & ears of sleepers to numb them, while
they delicately peck   out their eyes. They appear to spit
fine spray of nerve-   kill juice. Of a foggy A.M., one easily

spots them puffing   misty breath swirls over the dream-
bound faces: *wakers*   *go crawling for their lost eyeballs*
like so much loose   *change in cracks of the pavement . . .*

If research lab whiz   could isolate rat's gland extract,
an elusive chemical   blend, he'd strike it rich. No other
numbing potion works   so fast — Nature's own wild miracle

analgesic. Guyana   scams, cons, pickpockets — a breed
apart — take lessons   from these rats . . . *Your first night*
in Georgetown, says   Tony, *be on the lookout for ETHER*

MASK stalkers. They   scrounge about, and ambush the lone
hoofer in pairs: at   dusk, or just before dark, one grabs
your arms, the other   clamps the gauze pad on your cheeks

like a false second   face, or steel-mesh Catcher's Mask.
No antidote, once   you've taken a hit. Just hope, beg,
pray that they take   the mask off, soon after they fleece

you, pockets yanked   inside out, no farthing left behind
for a minibus fare . . .   Face down in the curb muck, the mask
still affixed, you   can die in two minutes. Maybe less.

One night, two muscly   teens jumped a luckless Security Guard
at Tower Hotel. Ether   Mask snuffed his brain — gaping mouth
prone on the Gauze,   he kept sucking it in until breath

quit. They'd broken   into all the rooms, robbed that place
silly, came away with   a record haul of jewels . . . No intent
to kill, but Ether's   more lethal than anyone'd guess. . . .

AGAINST NATURE TIMOTHY LIU

Eight dollars for a dozen roses sold
on Christopher and Grove where another

fag was hunted down last night by some
fraternity boys who took their turns

with a pocket knife — a Village safari
kicking the bias death toll up a notch

or two. Boytoy hothouse flowers forced
to bloom too soon — their eyelids ringed

with bruise. More and more undercover
cops unloading into streets where neon

lipstick-strutting sluts blow kisses far
and wide. As weed to crack, so blood

to thrusting hips in vacant lots where
pissed-on corpses mark a warring turf.

REVENGE, LIKE HABANERO PEPPERS RACHEL LODEN

The law I love is major mover
— Robert Duncan

Revenge, like habanero peppers, clears
the sinuses, presses the errant

sweetness into every flower. I'd swear
the trees were giddier than usual

today, all that leaf-glitter trembling
to give away such money. I graze, oh

I shall graze long and affectionately
on the fiefdom I survey, though I am

no seashell-gatherer, nor do I wander
cluelessly among the darling buds

of May (etc., etc.). On this plane
for the duration: loyal and doddering

like some old stooped family retainer
with a plot-twisting identity, I remain

the rhapsodist of cunning, blithering
songbird of iniquity, and while-u-wait

the law I love moves through here
like a wall of fire, and it is leaving

everything exactly as it stands, and
saving nothing standing in its wake.

RECONSTRUCTED FACE RACHEL LODEN

Surely this face — generic, blank —
betrays no terror. But her other face
is lost and floating on the river,
upturned like a lily in the air.

The police artist has slapped the flesh
back on her, wants us to know her,
makes her smile in that special way
a reconstructed woman smiles

after she's found without her face on
in a river, as though she tried
but failed to save us from the trouble
of her being there, our having to admit

that yes, we know her, smiling in the clay
the way we know the face of our own mother,
the reconstructed face that never
fooled us, built as crudely as it was

upon the scaffold of the other.

SHALL WE GATHER AT THE RIVER? MONIFA LOVE

for Mirtha

Beneath the machete we close our eyes
we see the blades our skin
a sea-red tryst
we open hissing
and our jolted anatomies curl into prayer
and confession.
You rub your remembering fingertips
I have become a kite
I see it from afar
the past.

This is the story you bring me.
You press it
into my hands
as if I can hold it.
As if I want it.
As if I can drink from it
and not grow small.

HATE CRIMES JOANNE LOWERY

When I hold the prison warden's face underwater
there's a kind of mauve around his amazed eyes
I find beautiful.

And when I take a 2 × 4 and bash
the face of a homophobic evangelist
the results look good enough for a McDonald's
Double Cheeseburger, no mustard.

Now that God has died, who will forgive
my desire to remove the anti-anti-christ?

I am so weary of being right.
Things could be a tad or two better.
My neighbor deserves the opposite of love,
and that, that I can give.

CHIVALRY JOHN LUNDBERG

Some nights, the girl heard scales scrape
the floor, as the slow, heavy body
dragged itself through the kitchen,
with its red eyes and acrid breath,

into her parents' bedroom. And the yells
and screams would start, a crash
behind the wall. She hid in the sheets
like her father said; the fights never lasted long.

Mornings, her mother would smile through a bruise,
sweep up the pieces of a lamp. And Dad,
too tired to talk, took his coffee in a thermos,
kept his eyes down.

How could she not be proud of him?
The bright iron armor he slept in,
the white sword he kept beside the bed.
He stood between them and what came in the dark.

The next night, he'd come home with tears
in his eyes, roses clutched to his chest.
He'd hold her with the strongest arms, the hero;
he was always home when the dragon came.

I STILL CAN'T SAY THE WORD   WALT McDONALD

Simply sit still, if you must, and breathe.
Breathe in and let it out. Again. See how
the seconds crawl. Mumble the word you feel.
Or scream, yes, scream, beat wood, strip the flowers,

break the table if you must. But not your fist.
All right, your fist, then; if it breaks, it breaks.
That's good. No one can hold her breath like this
or beat a table like a metronome. Today

is almost dark, tomorrow will be gone.
We'll look back Saturday and call each week
tomorrow. Curse cars and alcohol
again, damn all drunk drivers, scream and shriek.

I'll never blame, no matter what you do.
Guns can't bring him back. I'd take this gun
and pistol-whip his face to jam, for you,
I'd break his bones and suck the marrow and blood

like siphoning raw gas, and spit the platelets
out, if that would save you. I'd skin him
like a deer and stitch it like a shield, if that
would bring back our boy, leap arm-locked with him

into the fire myself, if our son could live.
I've said it and I mean it, but it's bald
as a lie. The facts are we are home, like this
together, grieving, and our son is gone.

SMOKESTACKS, CHICAGO CAMPBELL McGRATH

To burn, to smolder with the jeweled incendiary coal
of wanting, to move and never
stop, to seize, to use,
to shape, grasp, glut, these united
states of transition, that's
it, that is it,
our greatness, right
there. Dig down the ranges, carve out
rivers and handguns and dumps, trash it,
raze it, torch
the whole stuck-pig of it. Why
the fuck not? Immediately I am flying
past some probable
pickup truck with undeniable motor
boat in tow, a caravan
of fishermen no less, bass and bronze eucalyptus scars,
red teeth of erosion click-clacking
their bitterness. And
the sports fans
coming home through a rain
of tattered pompons. And the restless
guns of suburban hunters shooting
skeet along the lake. Desire is
the name of every vessel out there, but
I think the wind that drives them
is darker. I think I see
the tiny sails are full of hate
and I am
strangely glad. Don't stop,
hate and learn to love your hatred,
learn to kill and love the killing of what you hate,
keep moving,
rage, burn, immolate. Let the one
great hunger flower
among the honeysuckle skulls
and spent shells
of the city. Let longing
fuel the avenues of bowling alleys and flamingo
tattoos. Let sorrow glean the shards

of the soul's bright jars
and abandoned
congregations. Harvest moon
above the petrified
forest of smokestacks.

VINCENT PETER MEINKE

One time Vincent snapped Melinda's arm
like a chopstick though really
she broke it herself trying to pull out
of his fat beige fingers wrapped
almost double around her skinny wrist

We were kids and we poked and tortured
Vincent because he was fat   slow   and different
towering over us   his face from another planet
green and slack   his talk a whine
we couldn't translate   Our parents told us

Let him alone!   and I sometimes think
if we had only obeyed them   Melinda and I
might have been happy   I suppose even
children should pay for their sins   *but Vincent*
we're sorry   please forgive us   Her arm is fine

RAGE PETER MEINKE

Eighteen below: the black-capped chickadee
bangs on the suet in front of the cat
pressing against the pane. The woodpile
sprawls below the porch, the woodsmoke shadow
solid as the snow, the emptiness
where the old elm used to be — all frozen forever
in this scene, by these words, on this page:
a poor farmhouse broken down by age.

And rage, too, will never go away, never;
your disappointment, bitter as ash, more
murderous than this weather,
is part of what we'd taste like now
if whatever's in the woods got in the house.
You're sleeping now: you never had it better.

[THE MAN WHO MELTS . . .] DONALD MORRILL

The man who melts a plastic garbage bag
into a dagger, this inmate fearing other inmates,
has a point to make, a mark.
He understands a different courtesy
than we who read of his self-reliance
in a magazine designed to move.
Who deserves the conviction in this artificer?
His innocence and ours persist beyond dispute.
To sneak it back to the daily cell,
its rumpled black edge like a brittle flint —
to know it's ready there —
secures the world and reforms the times.
Go through his pockets, you won't find it.
Frisk your soul, someone's relative as well,
and think of decency, of vengeance and empathy.
Think of the chances at lights out.

SALEM, INDIANA, 1983 RICHARD NEWMAN

That summer my best friend Matt and I manned
the wheel of his father's 4WD red
pick-up through the fields and clumps of trees
and down the sudden turns of the Indiana
backroads to the family farm of his boyhood.
We loved the freedom of driving anywhere

and more the lie of speeding off to nowhere.
In the rush he told me his grandpa was a Klansman
one summer — how in all likelihood
Matt had found the faded, reddened
photograph of the last Indiana
lynching: a man hanging from a tree,

how it looked like the same slippery elm tree
he climbed as a kid, he didn't remember where.
A black family moved to Salem, Indiana,
and the neighbors descended on this one man,
flayed his skin from black to sticky red.
Matt's grandma sewed the white sheets and hoods.

He told me once how at a neighborhood
picnic his uncle took him under a shadetree
(It wasn't long ago, and Matt turned red
with shame.) and said, *We don't care where
they go. We have nothing against the Black Man —
We just don't want him here in Indiana.*

We finally made it to Salem, Indiana,
and as if to underlie the truth or falsehood
of Matt's story, there was the old man,
either sleeping or staring at the trees,
sitting on the back porch in his underwear,
his hair still a burnished copper red,

his arms and neck freckled and farm-reddened
from working the soil of the silty Indiana
fields. His socks were bunched and wrinkled where
they slumped below his ankles. I pictured the hood

over his nodding head, the whipping tree.
Where lay the cruelty to his fellow man?

Just a tired old fart in his underwear,
resigned to withering manhood, watching the red
sun burn below the Indiana treeline.

TALLAHASSEE AIMEE NEZHUKUMATATHIL

This whole town is sand. Even the cypress
don't seem to care — brush beards of moss
dangle on rough limbs, hang float-like, their job.
It's only 10 o'clock and my clothes already soaked
under this sun, my shoes scuff the pathetic tufts
of grass trying to grow in this sandsoil. If you kick
at the green long enough, you'll hit a cloaked beach,
a time of transparent things: Conquistadors scraping
the sand for delicious water, feather-red bobs
of their helmets fierce in the sun, decades of orange farmers
pulling the sand for weeds. With these two men holding
my hands against a rusty chainlink fence, pressing
their dog mouths to my chest and damp neck, grains fly
from my toe. My pulse is still quick, though I am casual,
scanning the lake for spindly birds, a turtle. For days
a steady throb in my left ear has left my fingertips
cold, as if the beat in my ear sends a weird music,
makes what I touch now — a waxy leaf, a fruit
from my pocket — chilled, not real.
My heart races, I focus instead on a waterbug
bouncing its delicate legs on a swampy bubble.
Nothing calms me; I can still hear them.

REGARDLESS OF THE FINAL SCORE DEBRA NYSTROM

— Pierre, South Dakota

At Homecoming we cheered for game's-end,
when the king and queen appeared
in eagle feathers and buck-skin:
hundreds of palms drumming bleachers
as the royal pair lifted a torch-pole,
and flames snapped along gasoline-soaked
rags wrapping the goal-posts.
We left them to burn, weaving
the snake-dance down Main Street then —
a school of white kids flinging themselves
along the dark, as if some current they couldn't
understand passed through them, like the impulse
of the show-horse Sitting Bull had accepted
from Buffalo Bill: when Lakota followers
crossed police who came to arrest the old chief,
the rattled animal sat upright, raised
one hoof as it had been taught,
fluttered its mane and rose to pace out
all the tricks it knew began with gunshot.

THE INTRUSION BILJANA D. OBRADOVIČ

— Lincoln, Nebraska

My landlord called at 11:00 P.M.,
too late for discussing my rent, I thought.
　But he wanted someone to talk to,
and I was the only tenant who could listen
　to his frightened voice, understand
why he couldn't go to sleep after
　a Vietnamese pushed himself inside
Mel's house, as if it were his own,
　sat on the couch, as if he had been there before,
and had always placed himself in that spot;
　after the stranger, with booze on his breath
hugged Mel, as if they were old buddies;
　after Mel somehow, half an hour later,
persuaded this man with whatever sign language
　he could use, and the few English words
the man spoke, for him to please, leave.
　Mel's Ph.D. in Modern Languages didn't help,
how could he have known to study Vietnamese
　instead of Spanish and German?
I gave him a scotch on the rocks, to cool him off;
　this town, too small for crime, he had thought,
now he knows it wasn't small enough —
　he could have been killed, and
I had my windows opened, didn't hear anything.
　My student told me he had a house full of guns,
told me I should own one, just in case —
　I said, "I'm sure you have some to spare!"
I couldn't kill anyone, but last night
　I kept all windows, doors, locked.
I had run away from a big city,
　but the city was catching up.

MARY MIHALIK ED OCHESTER

She'd tried to kill herself before.
Six kids, no money.

She was drunk
they said, doing 80, 90

on the slick blacktop
twisty and at dusk, and they

said there were no skidmarks
where she sailed under

the coal truck going slow
uphill out of the crossroad and

sheared the top of her Chevette
clean off and the rumor was

that when the cops came,
in the back seat they found her head.

People said all she needed
was a job, and I guess they're right.

And probably everyone thought
she needed love but everybody

says you've got to earn that,
though I think love's a gift,

the way money is for some, who
have a lot and never earned it.

I don't know. But a few nights later
when I walked past there, the insects

were at their cheerful static.
Aside from them the woods were silent.

And there were fireflies.

BLOOD WILLIAM OLSEN

Sometimes blood looks for an opening,
any way to get out from under us and the knives.
Blood cuts into blood to look and its hands grasp blood.
My block is a corral of yellow crime scene tape.
Twenty cop cars —
sometimes blood looks at blood for an explanation.
It turns out the whole block slept through a murder.
A social worker was stabbed by her psychotic charge
not two houses down, near the door of the Headstart School,
where the underprivileged play catch-up next door to the door
    to the School for the Disabled.
Both schools are underfunded, with all their school-day lives.
Call us childish, call us to our teachers:
a cop with a clipboard calls me over, to ask me what of blood I
    heard.
He knows in his blood better than to say it that way.
He puts it neutrally, may his heart feel adjudged by restraint,
may the differently abled be restrained for their own good,
and when I say *his* "heart" may I mean *mine* and may my mouth feel
    antique —
what he asks me is if I heard any cries — no, not even that,
    just . . . "anything."
Let's get this right.
Does a dying self make up a face as it goes, will any face
    do?
Right there on the concrete a bloodstain the children will pass,
    to touch it:
what's to touch once blood stops doing its cartwheels?
Someone has stepped out from under our thumbs and heels?
I wish I had a heart that would take care of . . . what?
Can anyone ever make blood do anything? Can clouds
    be pushed around?
On and on till the questions are all open coffins.
Sleepy me, a cop, a schizo the state sent packing
and a dead do-gooder the papers will leach till her photo
    is a window after death.
By the windows of institutional ministration the cop
glances away from me at wheelchairs, spokes aglitter
like Ezekiel's chariot about to commence his convictions.
God cares that our families and homelands are slaughtered for being
    weak.

We are all victims, down to the butchers among us?
Weakness has strength, even if it hasn't killed us?
Coffins.
I drive by these windows each day, some strapped in
    headgear,
others who can be trusted to walk careen from wall
    to wall —
one always laughs with a "it's not funny" lodged in his laugh;
another always carries a Raggedy Ann doll with a sewed
    smile
and button eyes hanging by threads,
the stuffing coming out of it, affection has mauled it —
she holds tight what even oblivion gave up torturing,
clouds shining, her wheelchair passes me, a cop and our laws
    and our clue, blood;
its driver squints smiling into a happiness that is its own
    skewed warding of us off,
her wheelchair shines — O steel throne — a fool might even believe
she would wish to reign over our disabling kingdom.

HAPPY AS I AM STEVE ORLEN

Trailer parks, projects, Circle K parking lots,
And trash-ridden vacant places,
And coldly illuminated side streets with front porches
Peeling their rented paint. He's sullen. She's screaming. Two fat babies
Sit dazed on a couch. There's maybe a knife or a gun, and blood,
A few drops already scabbing on her face or pooled dry
On the sidewalk, mapping a wound, and it's always afterwards,
Ten minutes later, a half hour.

                                   Every night I watch the show *Cops*
After dinner. I'm by myself because it upsets my wife, the voyeurism
Of it, the high-pitched, tension emergency sounds,
And my son, a good boy who by now has fallen far from the tree,
Hates the unpredictability, the chaos, and blood, *especially the blood*,
He says, but he loves the verbal violence of *rap* music, so who knows
How far he's fallen,

                      and I love the opening *rap* song, "Bad Boys,"
Because that's what I thought I always was, what my father called me
As a boy, the neighbors, too, the relatives, the principal of the junior
     high
Who told my father on the phone, *You don't have to worry about*
Your son going to college, he's going to jail, and hung up.

Why do you watch that stuff? my wife asks from the kitchen.
Because I feel I sort of *know* these people, from childhood —
The perps, the cops, the victims —
Especially when the show the smaller cities,
Like the one I grew up in, Holyoke, Massachusetts, which is not
This TV city in fact, so the show is both real and not real
And I can believe whatever I want. I'm waiting to see
Someone I used to know, one of the screw-offs, the junior high
Falling-down-drunks, the burglars, window-smashers, car stealers,
Famous street fighters, the greater and the lesser clowns, those in
     groups
And those mysterious maniacs who work alone. Those people gathered
On the television porch, still arguing, the very sullen, bare-chested man
In close-up with SUGAR tattooed over one nipple and CREAM
Over the other, and the very frightened, dispossessed-looking
Plump woman biting her nails, and through the screen door
Three children asleep on a couch, crumpled like pieces of dropped
     paper
Nobody notices, and the cops — I think if I look closer

I'll recognize one of them.
                              I know
I know that woman smothered in light on the front porch
Because I went out with her once.
Actually, I sat next to her *doppelganger*
In *The Victory Theatre* on one of those Friday nights
When all the kids went to the movies in summer.
Her name was always *Bunny*
Or *Beverly*, one sitting on my right and one on my left,
Shadows only, in profile, and after the opening credits
I put my arm around Bunny's shoulder and we started kissing,
And then I felt her up. I didn't know her. I couldn't even
Quite see her face, but I liked the slow glow of her, and the girl-smell
Of her rose petal soap, and the way her girlfriend nibbled
At her cuticles and watched us instead of the movie,
Until I turned to her and we went at it, too, back and forth like that.

And now she — Beverly, Bunny, I can't tell — is on TV,
Famous for several minutes in a humiliating scene, almost live
And pretty much unedited, with a long slash on her right cheek
And a smudged bump on her pale forehead, and she seems —
Not happy, of course — but *in* it, in her life,
While one cop is taking notes on a pad and another
Is frisking the squirming man, asking
Do you have any needles in your pockets, sir?

Someone you can't see is filming the whole slow chaos
With an unsteady hand, panning to
The small crowd gathered like a chorus in their night-clothes,
And the red lights twirling, surveilling. The cops are being nice to
      everyone.
They're used to this. They know they're on TV. They've taken courses
In courtesy. With a bit of bad luck or a wrong turn taken
It could have been them being frisked and cuffed on some Hillside
      Avenue.

Sometimes, proudly, I tell my son stories
About burglaries at "midnight lumber," the one siren coming in,
Then the voices exploding at us like those inchers on the Fourth of
      July,
The running, scrambling over back fences, hiding, the whispered
      laughing,
While the cops looked for us desultorily, though if caught

We would get a smack or two.

                                        The woman is mumbling something
We can't hear in our living rooms. I *know*
She is either Beverly or Bunny, though whatever was glowing about her,
Whatever innocence comprised her being,
Has dimmed to a cold illumination
On a front porch. Somebody in me is hearing her say,
Hey, Turk — they used to call me Turk — *Why don't you
Come out and join us,* or *Why are you out there
And I'm in here on your television set?* Or *Are you happy in your life?*
Actually, she's laughing, mildly, inaudibly, at her situation of this night.
It's just life. *Everybody's life is just life, right?* she seems to be saying.
And *Some nights you're in the chorus and some nights
You're in the middle of the mess, right?*

                                        My wife
Has put the cookies out to cool. To some *rap*
My son is break-dancing for me, interrupting my favorite show,
Irritating me on purpose. *How do you like that move?* he asks.
It's a good one, pal, I tell him, very happy with how he's turning out,
But wondering, stupidly, why he's not like me, out in the street
Getting into trouble, and wondering why I'm watching strangers on TV,
Peeping through a keyhole into the alternate universe.

Happy as I am, happy as anyone is, I still have this urge
To be with Beverly tonight, with Bunny, too.
Not on that front porch, but in the chorus
Where not a word is spoken.
Not thinking much. Only the body's chemical fuming.
Only a movie theater where half the kids are necking
Furiously and the other half watching, and Bunny and Beverly and I
Are touching each other in a twisted, anonymous passion
Within the smells of Beverly's soap, the cigarette smoke in Bunny's
Endlessly long brown hair, their urgent sweat, their lips, their lipstick,
The overly sweet candy everyone around us is sucking on.

HOSTAGE DIXIE PARTRIDGE

Parents cluster across the street,
behind a scalloped rope and the neutral faces
of two young troopers. In the watched
windows of the school, barricaded with desks:
a shadow of movement — maybe only reflection,
a tree's wavering leaves.

Behind every parent's eyes, behind images
of guns and homemade bombs, a child-face
and body: thin wrist, a cowlick,
changing profile where new front teeth
seem suddenly adult.

A head moves past the barricade
at library windows: a tangible current crosses
from the crowd. Dry leaves are held in chain link
like folded notes. The iron outcry
of the recess bell swells through the playground.

THE PERSISTENCE OF MEMORY,
THE FAILURE OF POETRY ROBERT PHILLIPS

In 1979, a New York high school music student,
Renée Katz, was pushed in the path of a subway train.

The severed hand flutters
     on the subway track,
like a moth. No —

it is what it is,
     a severed hand.
It knows what it is.

And all the king's doctors
     and all the king's surgeons
put hand and stump together

again. Fingers move,
     somewhat. Blood circulates,
somewhat. "A miracle!" reporters

report. But it will only
     scratch and claw, a mouse
behind the bedroom wall. We forget.

At four A.M. the hand
     remembers: intricate musical
fingerings, the metallic

feel of the silver flute.

AFTER THE FACT: TO TED BUNDY ROBERT PHILLIPS

1.
The thing of it was,
you looked so handsome
and trustworthy —
such a nice smile.

The thing of it was,
you showed me
a laminated ID card,
said you were Police.

The thing was, you see,
I was seventeen,
didn't know people
could buy fake IDs.

Thing of it was,
you told me someone
had been arrested
breaking into my car,

did I want to go
down to the station
and press charges?
You'd drive me.

You had a hot car,
smooth, brand new.
Smelled like leather,
a turn-on. Like you.

2.
Not far down the road
you pulled over,
quickly handcuffed me,
unzipped yourself,

started waving a pistol.
You said you'd blow
my brains all over
the highway if I didn't

do what I was told.
Whatever the reason, I didn't
think you would.
(Your cock was tiny,

soft as a slug.) Somehow
I got the door open,
ran. You didn't fire,
but came after me

waving a tire jack.
I wore high heels,
couldn't run fast.
Thought I was a goner.

Then a VW came along.
I lifted my handcuffed
hands and hollered.
It stopped for me.

3.
I'm one of the lucky few.
I've seen your picture
in all the newspapers.
No question, it was you.

I've seen your face
most nights in dreams,
big as the harvest moon,
grinning like a goon.

It's the good-looking
ones I distrust the most —
the way they try to
sweet-talk their way.

Last week in a bar,
a guy walked over,
touched my shoulder.
In the ladies' room

I puked my guts out.
I'll find one so homely
someday, I'll simply
go along with him. Okay?

Fifteen years after,
you finally got fried.
Clean-shaven bastard,
inside me you're still alive.

BLOSSOM STANLEY PLUMLY

And after a while he'd say his head was a rose,
a big beautiful rose, and he was going to blow it
all over the room, he was going to blast blood.

And after a while he'd just put his head in his one good
hand the way children do who want to go into hiding.

I still can't get the smell of smoke from the woodstove out of my head.
A woman is frying bacon and the odor is char and sour and somebody
running a finger over your tongue. All those dead years and the grease

still glue on the wall. In Winchester, Virginia, the year the war
ended, the blacks were still dark clouds. My uncle had a knife
pulled on him holding his nose.

                              When the Guard marched eleven
German prisoners of war down from Washington they marched them
right through town, and it was spring and a parade like apple blossom.
Black and white, we lined up just to watch.

I still can't get the smell of apples out of my head —
trees in orchards all over the country, like flowers in a garden.
The trees the Germans planted that spring looked like flowers,

thin as whips. Even so the branch of a full-grown apple tree
is tested every summer: when I didn't watch I picked along with
every black boy big enough to lift a bushel. Frederick County.

The National Guard in nineteen forty-five was my father and any
other son who stayed home. Next door the father of my friend
had been home two long years, one arm, one leg gone. He was

honorary. He was white sometimes, and black, depending.
He was leaf and woodsmoke and leaning always into the wind.

And everybody called him Blossom because of the piece of apple
he kept tucked at the side of his mouth. When he was drinking
he'd bring his bottle over and talk to my father about Germans.

They go down, he'd say, they all go down on their guns.

Each five-petaled flower on the tree means an apple come summer.
I still can't get the bourbon smell of Blossom out of my head.
He spits his apple out and shoots himself in the mouth with his finger.

THE MAN IN MIAMI KEVIN PRUFER

Sometimes my sister calls to say
she's seen that man again
following fifty feet behind her on the street,
hiding his head when she looks, or
sitting only a few café tables away,
pretending to read, or
pacing in his camouflage jacket
outside her window.
Other times she hasn't seen him
in a day. What am I supposed to say?
Walk a different way to work,
stay with a friend, call the police,
come home?
I've said it all, the man won't go.

It doesn't snow where my sister lives,
and it's always two hours later.
Here the days are cold. It grows dark
earlier each evening. When she calls
it is twenty years ago and she has slipped
into my room. She nudges me awake;
she whispers in my ear:
it is our grandfather come for a visit,
it is our grandfather waiting
by the stairs. I used to look.
There was never anyone there.

My sister says: that doesn't matter.
That doesn't matter at all. What matters
is that crazy man who will not let me alone.

She does not know how long
the man has followed her.
Six weeks, or eight?
She saw him first a month ago.
He sat on the hood of her car
in his camo jacket and black sunglasses.
He nodded, as if to say hello,
then rose and ambled down the busy street.

As a girl, she saw many things
that were not there: Birds
circling above her bed, and, later,
tiny figures swinging from the curtains.
Sometimes it was some kind of devil
rocking on his hooves
over by the bedroom door. Our mother
took her to the doctor, who told her:
these things aren't real, they can't hurt you.
Sleep with the lights on.

Here, it won't stop snowing.
Each evening, everything is buried again,
and the icicles are heavier.
The man in Miami hasn't touched her,
so no one can do a thing.
If he doesn't touch her, no one can know a thing.

THE PYROMANIAC WYATT PRUNTY

A one-story is disheartening,
Brief unelaborated light building
Under eaves, traveling sideways, gulping air,
And the slow smoke bellying after.
Three stories, four, five, or more work best
For my hushed start, in which the rest
Becomes a climbing fall toward light,
The blue flame's leap to furnace white
And stoked accumulation where
Hunger lives on hunger, hollowing air
As the dicing flames still time,
As empty coats, arms bent in pantomime,
Go up, as my two shoes tip up, their toes
Curled the way I make whole buildings go —
Out of the rich gas and fire's brief bright
Dancing its combustible light
On top of light, as if it drew
The nail-board-mortar of all lives into
One hot cumulus billowing from below.
That's why I strike the match, that I may know
No god's revenge for fire, but my own,
My own curled side bent to a stone
As obdurate and blank as hate,
Although not for some dark bird's appetite,
I have my own of that, instead the flame,
Consuming everything the same
Till nothing offers more of hope
Than gas-soaked rags, the building smoke
That hides its fire so rising whole
Bright tongues curl into coals
As air shafts roar and windows amplify
How high my hungry bright will bite the sky.

TEDDY LEROY V. QUINTANA

We were walking down Central downtown,
and Teddy said to me, the way older guys
say something when teaching you this and that,
said don't give the Anglo girls the eye,
the satisfaction.
He turned me on to Cannonball, Bird, Brubeck: Time Out.
When I returned from Vietnam, he played
Bach's "Minuet in G Minor" for me on his rock 'n roll guitar
then put on "Love for Sale"
and smiled to himself, entranced
as he played it over, over, over, and over.
Next day I didn't have to read past the *Tribune* headlines
to know it was he who had beaten
his mother to death with a hammer in 5/4 time.

187 LEROY V. QUINTANA

In California there are one hundred and eighty-seven reasons
for a beating. Everything about you is illegal except your hands.
May they move fast, move fast, then move on.
Pray for rain.

who would
listen for what goes bump in the

goes boom in the morning a father

a man I know takes bombs apart for
a living bomb disposal being

a modern way to live with
fear   you

need merely be careful
my father said pay attention boom

in the night fire in the hole
another of those adult cold mornings

& the light is warily silver someone
feels better someone lives well

most delicate mode wish for the past
a past which with

care & cunning could be made to work
to order

this is a dream a past that works
as the present is an edge slicing

mind into sagital sections
as if

a formula   flies thrown through the
air arced   adhesion of

things attach to   fact   there is real
& there is not not   is a

difference   the imagined is a kind
of real   memory too

there was
a day I   was a small child

running among the legs of a father a grand
father   a brother   an uncle

I was praised for youth the war was over

nothing needed   exploding explaining
the tropical   the weeds of the pasture

the cows   distant   the future

distant   the line of trees   beyond
which the murk of water & cypress

knees rising   this was

& white egrets distant   once
became hats   entire birds dead

to adorn   shot for two feathers

mon panache   it was a time
gone who cares

nothing to it

what child not   me would
listen for what bump in the night

that goes boom in the morning

my father took bombs apart for the war
disposal being   a part of valor

a most modern way to
be careful my

father said   *pay your own way*   attention
in the night   fire in the hole

pain   not counting loneliness
a moment of terror for instance a sound of braking

& over the rise of the interstate one truck
turned sideways floating into your rear-view mirror

a clarity a dialogue with self
in which the possible passes

this is not interesting
I thought that if I could put it all down, that would be one way — John Ashbery

picture here

a cottage an adequate estate something
to live on pretty et cetera you cannot

see it to hear is possible the birds & some cows
lowing in the distance   slow sloe-eyed cows

in the distance

what   (if a house be built beside
still water in the evening fowl descend

awkward in their way to settle raucously
walking on water then sinking comfortable

in their element) happens next no one
knows what happens next

the spectacular this evening
great streak of purple heavy against cold

golden light the result of refraction clouds
frame the event give it depth

in time at the moment   *(after all, who won*

of the light going the color   *the Peloponnesian War?*
deepens beyond bearing will

touch with such magnificence you feel   *& how many died?*
your own future collapse sweetly

                                                . . . all of them
to tell the truth in time   Cows   *about the past find*
are warm walls & patient

try to remember the names   *its implication for the future*
lean your head against her flank   *anywhere but here*

the reverberating breath & the chewing   *now here = nowhere*

the deepening din   *in time)*
that sound

the horns of a cow are one kind of danger
memory is the other

I would once I did I could   make as we say
love & she was   there among the two

of us   It was a world   & home or might

as well have been   to climb limbs
like that to insert the self   in flesh

to live as if we were not   dying in tandem could
we   did we

what memory will do to the past   is too funny
for words

there are pleasures   a clean light intrudes

there are ways to know
a memory fell through him as clear light falls on herbs — Anne Carson

you have felt it usually pain   it was harder

to be a child than anyone knew   you were
who wasn't   it fell through him

I should have remembered the war it happened
two years before my birth

a stronger mind would remember   dismembering
the crustaceous   whose arrogant apathy

fills the void what armed creature
this was was recalled   called to the boy

she stood in the doorway   the boy did not heed
hear   she loved him he   remembers her his mother

a shadow   a map of me
on the world the wall one dimension   lost

o woe   *Suddenly everything is beautiful. He begins to cry* — Russell Edson
because it hurts   because it doesn't

the numbers don't add up   or they do
because Mom should be sent

to a home   because she refuses to go
because she smears the good rug

with dung   perhaps her own   perhaps the dog's
because there is a war

because there is no war   which would teach the young
what life is   that it's hard &

political   Cry because during the second world war
the zoo in Tokyo starved

its animals   what recourse
what if Americans bombed

liberated lions elephants like cows
would wander the footpaths

the theory of everything says   some things are continuous
some are discrete   contentment

is knowing the difference
if there is a difference

nothing is what it used to be   or is
the sunset is not fleeting

it is continuous & absolute   the only one
the one which has been happening

ever since the earth solidified out of a ring

of debris   even before that the ring
of debris refracted sunlight

into constituent wavelengths
including the ultraviolet   the infrared

which we so want to see it is just there beyond the edge
if the world hates you

know that it has hated me   *John 15:18*
before you   if the world

loves you you're on your own
"After clinging to their foreclosed chicken ranch

for two years, two women gave up the fight
and killed themselves and all their pets

just before the marshals seized the property"   — *Associated Press*
for a week the undiscovered bodies lay

in the garage. Thelma
J. Lee, 67, & Maureen R. O'Boyle, 51,

asphyxiated   three dogs on the floor   twelve cats
in the pickup one in a shopping cart   *"What would happen if bombs*
                                        hit the zoo? If the cages were broken
In a Japanese picture book   *and dangerous animals escaped*
children would pass & the elephants   *to run wild through the city . . .*
                                        by command of the Army, all

stretched trunks through the bars begging   *of the lions, tigers*
anything it is forbidden to feed   *leopards, bears, and big snakes*
                                                          were poisoned . . ."
no one is forgiven   — *Faithful Elephants*, Yukio Tsuchiya

it is generally accepted that the domestication of cattle followed sheep, goats, pigs and dogs. Modern domestic cattle evolved from a single early ancestor, the aurochs . . . It is believed the last surviving member of the species was killed by a poacher in 1627 on a hunting reserve near Warsaw, Poland. — *"Breeds of Livestock" okstate.edu*

DEVIL BEATING HIS WIFE RON RASH

"The devil beating his wife,"
my uncle claimed if thunder
lingered after sky turned blue,
and what strikes memory most is
how matter-of-fact he spoke,
as if he'd seen it first-hand,
and maybe he had, those nights
his father did not even
need the excuse of liquor
to slap brassed leather across
his wife's arms, legs, until she
gave up, surrendered her face
so he could finish, and yet
never raised that belt against
my uncle, or even voice
as he explained to his son,
mid-beating, how a wife must
learn respect, a lesson taught
best like this, but my uncle
listened to the silence of
a mouth clotted shut by blood,
waited for adolescence
to muscle arms, for the night
he lessoned his father with
his own blood, threw him out
of the house, vowed to kill him
if he came back, words believed
for he never did. We love
such an ending so let it
end there, the night that bad man
skulked away, not years later
when my cousin raised his shirt,
showed me welts where the belt slashed,
done once, never before or
after to son, wife, or daughter
but done that one time as if
to give the devil his due.

FIRST GRADE LIAM RECTOR

Allen Newport, famous in the first . . . Allen, forever
Fixed in the first for me unless I see him, unlikely,
Ever again . . . Allen getting his butt kicked

At recess; at lunch one day two assholes hocking
Into Allen's bologna on white, two saucy boys
Unable to stop messing with cross-eyed, dazed

Allen, and lord how I did enjoy beating the living
Shit out of one of them later, at my leisure,
In the courtyard where we really got to know each other

In that grade, that era, that site of spitting and so much
Defeat rising out of a sandwich, that first of many schools
I went to getting to know Allen and the people like him,

The ones who come up to you when you first get somewhere.

OF VIOLENCE G. TRAVIS REGIER

It is not so easy to shoot a man
As the movies would make you think
But it is not so difficult either
When he is standing on your porch
And will not leave when you tell him to
But curses you instead
And you know he has been inside your house
Fucking your wife again
And you have an unregistered handgun
Under the seat of your car.

It is not so easy to shoot a man
But not so difficult either:
A man is a big target
And the gun, that perfect machine,
Does all the work.

COACH IN EFFIGY JACK RIDL

His daughter saw him first, hanging
from the maple that hung its old arms
over the house, his body
a stuffed sheet, his head blooming
from the rope that surrounded
his neck. In the morning's moonlight,
she read their name scrawled like a scar
across his chest. She
remembered the way his hands
held her years ago when,
bloodied from a fall, she'd let
the scream we all carry
go to him. He seemed to take it,
hold it in his own hands, then
give it back to the earth.
At those times, she had seen him
in his own eyes. Now, in the midst
of this losing season, she wants to
take this swollen sheet, hold it
in her arms, let the hands
that made it and the fists
that rose against it join, let them
all stand around her as she sings
the only song, as she
lets the head rest, lets
the heart give out.

RAINFALL PIANO LUIS J. RODRIGUEZ

I wish I could swallow music,
fill myself with drumbeats and rainfall piano.
— *Patricia Smith*

Filo walked out my door,
made it to the corner,
and got shot.
When I saw him at the hospital,
he looked up from the gurney,
bottles of fluid attached to his arms,
and grinned.
When Papo got hit three times with a .44
we thought he wouldn't make it.
He lost part of a finger
and still limps:
Now he's serving 40 years
at Stateville
accused of exacting revenge
on one of the dudes
who laughed at him.
I can hardly listen to music anymore,
to Patricia's rainfall piano
playing the keys of desire on a CD.
The gunfire is louder.
Recently somebody sprayed
the pre-kindergarten graduation
ceremony at the elementary school
down my street.
Nobody got hit.
The parents stood there
dumbfounded —
The children instantly
dropped to the ground.

REDNECK WITH HAIR ON HIS BACK PAUL RUFFIN

Standing here in his muscle shirt at the bar,
with hair on his back and chest
and tufted like the stuff of nests
in opposing crotches
of a too familiar tree,
he is little more than an upright ape
who has learned the alphabet.
With his woman he is not gentle,
preferring her in her anxious state,
taking her when he will, and
the children fear his thundering voice.

This, God's finest creation, whose
eyebrows now have drifted from his cheekbones
like continents over time until he sees clearly
between them with his dark eyes
and reasons well behind them
in that smoking vault of the brain
where he knows what women are made for
and when to come in from the rain.

ANGEL BENJAMIN ALIRE SAÉNZ

for Patricia (and the children forced to appear in her court)

Lost. Again. I chase a piece of
Paper on my always cluttered desk. I reach, pick up
The waiting phone, the numbers like a cherished line
From a favorite poem or prayer. I hear your secretary's
Voice as I pronounce your name. She knows it's me, your
Husband (my voice as known to her as the perfectly kept
Files on her desk). "She's in a hearing, Ben. I can pass
The Judge a note." "No, just tell her I — " My voice falls
Off as I hang up the phone. I know you are out of
Reach before I even call. I know you are at work, know you
Are sitting on the bench listening to another case, another
Sordid story of a child mangled like cars in a wreck.
How can you listen to these tales of fractured lives? Day
After day, you sit. You listen. Day after day, I call. You
Cannot speak to me. I can't keep myself from calling. A habit
I can't break. I glare at the phone, then continue my search
For that misplaced piece of paper. Thrown away, perhaps.
Thrown away? But I needed it. Careless. I'm so careless.

I walk back to my desk. I sit
And stare at the twelve photographs of you I framed and keep
So I can see you when you're somewhere else. I study
All the poses. I decide which look you're wearing at this
Moment of the day. I see you, sitting on your judge's bench.
Your face lights up the room, eyes as dark and shiny as your
Robe. I picture you scolding an unprepared lawyer. I picture
You asking the hundred difficult questions that must be
Asked. *Those marks — who put them there? Does this boy eat?* You
Do not shrink from your task. You have long since ceased
To be afraid. I picture you speaking with a child who's
Lived a life of fear. Love is as foreign to him as London
Or Madrid. I can hear your voice as you speak, soft
As a cloud floating across a droughted summer sky. I picture
The child answering your questions. I picture your eyes as
You listen. You hide your grief and rage. Your dark eyes know
A child is a miracle. *How could the world not know this?*
But the world does not have your eyes. Blindness
The disease of the twentieth century.

And then I picture
You and your Gabriela (my Gabriela, too). I hear your voices
Filling up the house. Your dark daughter leans into your
Shoulder *Mama, Mama*. I picture you saving her life. I
Picture you saving mine. Again, I stare at the twelve
Images of you, *my wife, my wife, mi vida*. My eyes fall on the
Image where you're smiling. Your black robe's turned to
White. A million children. Reaching out to touch. An angel.

PORCELAIN CHILDHOOD KATHERINE SÁNCHEZ

Death is patient as a chess set.
My black pawns are roach
corpses on kitchen tiles.

Mother, in a white dress, presents
the broom like a ceremonial staff.
She says: *The cycle of order*

from chaos can't be refused.
I am a chess player with a theory.
As Oedipus discovered,

Fate makes up the rules as she goes.
Mother reappears in the doorway
clutching my black queen

by the throat. The queen tells me:
Chaos must be played out.
Mother opens her hand.

A glass hand props against
a roach body. A woman's head
lies on its side, as if in sleep.

The queen is no longer
the queen. The head says: *Being whole*
is an illusion. Mother leaves the room,

her shadow diminishing on the wall
like a child. I sweep porcelain
into a garbage bag.

I save my queen's black eyes.
They stare up from my palm
like bullets.

THE TALKING CURE SHEROD SANTOS

> *No sadness*
> *Is greater than in misery to rehearse*
> *Memories of joy.*
> — Inferno

Eyes shut. Lapsed time. The 2 A.M. aquarium light.
The background noise of my parents' party
winding down upstairs. A suspended moment
between two worlds while the mind's uprooted
from a sleep that won't quite blink away,
and a woman from one of the other of those worlds
who has found her way beside my bed saying,
Shhh, shhh, it's only me, though I can't imagine
who *me* might be. And before I'm able to ask her,
she has passed a finger across my lips, unfastened
the topmost pearl-snap button on her ecru blouse
(the sound a flame makes touched to glass, the glass
then touched to water), and guided my hand
held trembling beneath the rustle of that enfolded cloth.
And in that still assembling hour, assembling now

through the same stirred waterlight that it did then,
I have felt for the first time in my life, have felt
as something inside of me, as another body within
my own, her breathing deepen, and its guttering.
Things aren't always what they seem to be,
and neither, I suppose, are the things we feel.
But the truth is I was scared to think that dream
might actually *be* a dream, or that, in turn,
it might prove not to be a dream at all, for it seemed
blood-bidden what happens then, when she eases
my hand to a place I can only conceive of as
a vacancy, a chill alongside that pillowed hillock
she'd moved it from. She draws it, you see, along
the raised abrasion of a surgical scar that cut
in a transverse angle from her rib cage to her shoulder.

And that, she whispers, is the reason she's come.
The reason she's left the party upstairs. The reason
she simply wants me now to look at her, wants me
just to look and see the body her husband refuses

to see. But could that really have happened?
I wondered about it even then. And what
could it have to do with tears? The tears that all
too readily come when she finally steps back
from my side, lets fall her blouse and underthings,
and stands there backlit by an aquarium glow
her body inflected with a sorrow that lay
well beyond the reach of my thirteen years.
And this is where I ask myself if all of this
was only a fantasy, just another freak,
enciphered scene unspooled from the bobbin

of an adolescent's dreams. Believing that,
my parents both earnestly stood their ground
the following fall, when her husband found her
four months pregnant, sprawled out naked
on the bathroom floor beside an emptied bottle
of Nembutal. I talked to people about it when
things came to light. One caseworker in particular
took the better part of an afternoon to explain
why it was the letters this woman and I exchanged
had nothing to do with love at all, not with
"real" love anyway, but with something more —
how did he put it? — "unnatural," I think, though
clearly he meant to say "perverse." I accepted that.
I saw the sense. But what I recall (and, admittedly,
it took me years to sort what's fact from fiction),

what I recall is that, as she stands there figured in
the pale aquarelles her ever-receding memory
paints, I swim out toward her to be taken up by
the current of her inclining arms, to be folded back
into another world where my own tears start,
though what I wept for I can't say — *that* is what
I remember. That and the more unlikely fact
that all of this happened even as she was somehow
muffling the sounds I could not keep down,
easing me under and taking me in, taking me into
the mind's all suddenly silvered light, and inside that
to a welling in the blood, a fullness in the heart,
the secret, solitary, nowhere of a place where in
one brief fluorescing stroke a shudder of grief
and arousal struck a lifelong, inwrought, echoing chord.

I can tell by the way you peer up over your glasses
that you're probably wondering why, in thirty-five years
of marriage, I never told my wife about any of this.
But let me ask you something, now that our hour
has come to an end, now that I've chattered on and on
while you, as usual, say nothing. Let me ask
if you and the others in your profession
don't sometimes feel like the ones to whom
it has devolved — from God, no less — to serve
as custodians for our souls? The ones who keep
from ravelling into oblivion that elaborate tapestry
of self-delusions upon which our community
now depends for moral and spiritual guidance?
No, I didn't think you'd answer that. You're right
not to, of course. Where were we then? Ah, yes,

the reason I haven't told my wife. It's simple really.
I just didn't want to hurt her. I know you'll say
my *not* telling her has hurt her more, but
it seems to me, despite the conventional wisdom,
some truths can do more harm than good. Or maybe
I've only come to feel, as time has passed,
that we understand less than we pretend about how
to love, or why we should, or when it's right,
or what we ought to expect from it. And who's to say,
given the passionless affections, the pent-up malice
and forbearance with which most couples tend to treat
each other for the better part of their married lives,
who's to say that what I had with that poor woman
years ago wasn't actually love of a finer kind
than I've known since, or am ever likely to know again?

FILM NOIR ARAM SAROYAN

He was too excited to fall asleep.
The little dog wouldn't stop barking.
He took out his gun.
He took out his handkerchief.
He took out his notebook.
He drank his coffee and left a dime.
He walked into the room.
He took her in his arms.
She let him in and walked out of the room.
He ran down the escalator.
He left the motor running.
He waited in the rain.
He needed something to tell the police.
He went down unconscious.
The blood drained from his face.
His eyes melted into a smile.
He dialed and waited, looking around.
He took off his hat in the elevator.
He rang the doorbell and waited.
He poured the cereal and added milk.
He opened the refrigerator and looked in.
He turned the page and continued reading.
He shut the door and switched the light on.
He looked up at a plane in the sky.
He put three pennies one on top of another.
He squeezed onto the elevator.
He took out his key.
He helped her into her coat.
He crossed the room and picked up the phone.
He drove on through the heavy rain.
He whistled for a cab.
He turned the corner and bumped into her.
She gradually surrendered to his kiss.
He drove past the wrought-iron gates.
He lit a cigarette and waited.
He lied to the police.
He threw the dice and won.
He folded the newspaper and crossed his legs.
He sat down in the lobby.
He tied his shoes and stood up.

He put on his hat but didn't get up.
He thought about her until he fell asleep.
He said "Goodbye" and hung up.
He threw the dice and lost.
He dialed and waited for her to answer.
He left some money for her.
He looked for her door number.
The police arrived late.
He walked into her building.
He let her do the explaining.
He gave up hope and begged.
He locked his car and walked.
She gave him that look of hers.
He put a finger to his lips.
He wiped his mouth and left.
He slapped her across the face hard.
He lit a cigarette in the dark.
The police wouldn't understand.
Her little dog slept.
Her voice had an edge to it.
Her hands were wonderful when she touched him.
His mind might be playing tricks on him.
The low hills reminded him of her.
There was no way to cut his losses.
He needed a shave and a haircut.
The coffee did nothing for him.
She was somewhere else when he called.
Pain stabbed him as he reached toward the glove compartment.
He needed a little time in the desert.
He decided to head for the beach and then thought better.
He needed about $5,000.
He ran out of Luckies and crumpled the pack.
He left his hat on in the car.
Maybe he was ready to die.
He checked his wallet pocket.
All of his friends had disappeared.
He remembered her naked body.
He had almost no savings.
He was at least ten pounds overweight.
He realized he was in love with her.

SOME POEMS AREN'T FOR YOU HEATHER SELLERS

When I think back now how my dad
hit a girl, a teenage girl, his knucklebone a rapids,
his own tears a simple and larger fucking up
I think how I went to see Holmie and went
to play blackjack back of the Amber Keg
and I pretended I wasn't the pink bleed, it wasn't
the heart. Because it was just my heart. Nothing
much happened to my skin, or his, or the frog
who lived in our kitchen, his peripetatic   soul
launches, grapefruit, soap dish, cutting board, melon,
the hanging basket where he lived,
where he hopped from, freeway of delight, green
freedom. We loved our kitchen frog, me and
my dad. I had a mouth. Though I didn't use it
for that. He was calm by then by gin, and propped
up. Underwear is truly fabulous. And me turning
eighteen and three inches taller — three inches is
a lot of span. It's a lot to have on a man. Quick I
learned how to pick my weddings, lose my battles,
telephone Holmie and to want
him, want to watch him making love to me.
I felt like I rhymed with him. I felt like a child's
tongue. I felt like I was the fist that lost the last lick
and down my throat I felt every syllable my father ever
burned or spattered there, I felt that. His breath, little bit
green. I loved him enough. Don't have to feel guilt, feel
what's coming fast to the face. What I see there
now is eyes if you stare hard enough a knuckle is
like a chin with a comet in it, if you clean something
you will kill what makes its house there and shouldn't.

WOLF SOUP VIJAY SESHADRI

In the version of the Three Little Pigs
that I've been given to read my child,
the first two pigs, after the wolf
has blown their houses down
("Little piggy, little piggy, let me come in"),
find refuge with their perspicacious brother.
The wolf, for his part, displays
no motivation, only an impulse arrested
from his body's churning electrolytes
to demolish architectural follies.
He doesn't chase and corner the pigs.
He doesn't have a grudge against
the race of pigs, nor is he in the mood
for pig's knuckles or a nice pig's-ear taco
or even a simple ham sandwich.
And when he comes down the chimney
of the third pig's house — the one
he can't blow down, the one made
of brick, with its dormer windows
tricked out in blue, their trim
decorated with orange daisies —
he suffers for his motiveless malignancy,
in the soup pot waiting for him,
the lid of which has been removed
with a timely flourish, nothing worse
than a scalding, and runs back
to his lair somewhere over the hill.
Everyone has survived their lessons.
Everyone, as in the Last Judgment
of the Zoroastrians, is saved,
even the wolf, today exterminated
across much of the world, and almost so
in the forty-eight contiguous states.
The real story, which is locked
in my desk while I write this encryption,
goes, as you all remember, differently.
In it, the wolf eats the first two pigs,
but the third pig, the smart pig,
the shrewd, shrewd little pig, eats him
in a soup flavored with the turnips

gathered in a memorable prior episode.
Long did that pig rest a pensive trotter
on the windowsill, as he looked down
the dusty road traveled by the wolf.
His brothers were dead, his mother
unapproachable in her grief, and for weeks
the taste of wolf, at once unguent, farinaceous,
brittle, and serene, touched his mind
with a golden fire. In a pig's eye, he thought,
as his molecules began to recombine . . .
My son might be ready for this version
of the story. Like most four-year-olds,
he's precocious and realistic and bloody-minded.
He already knows, for example, that Jack
was nothing better than a common thief,
and has at some point observed
that giants let their fingernails grow,
sometimes to hideous lengths.

A BIRTHDAY PARTY ON OLD ORCHARD ROAD

VIVIAN SHIPLEY

It's Fourth of July and for this one day to celebrate
freedom, it's okay to talk with our mouths full.

Hot dogs and chili are the prelude to salutes,
cherry bombs, lady fingers, Chinese. Clear prey

for crows, a beetle larger than a cockroach, gleaming
green then blue ventures onto the pink granite around

the pool — an error, though the bug's last. Civilization
means nothing now but to honor Washington, we debate:

let's get a Dixie Cup and blow him to bits; tie a bottle
rocket, send him aloft; gas him with a smoke bomb;

ignite him with a sparkler. Waltzing around, we lift
our arms to vote. We're a democracy. Attracted

by spiders about to kill ants, Darwin scribbled, *Efforts
which the poor little creatures made to extricate*

themselves from such a death were wonderful. No such
sport, our beetle ignores strings of fireworks, circling

like a necklace of coral laid flat. Five, four, three, two,
one, zero! Does the shock ripple his shell, bones rattling

as beans in a maraca do? Our need for sound, smoke
satisfied, we reel off statistics about drugs, inner city

violence, the New Haven father who burned two initials
on his son's forearm with cigarettes. We wonder why.

SLEEPING SOUNDLY WHERE
LIZZIE BORDEN DID VIVIAN SHIPLEY

From fields where glory does not stay
— A. E. Housman

Ambiguity, an unsolved murder case from a hot August day in 1892, has lured me. That and the chance to sleep in the bed of a thirty-two-year-old woman, and a Sunday school teacher at that, who might have taken an axe and killed her seventy-year-old father with ten blows to the head and her stepmother with nineteen. Lizzie is the only Fall River woman modern and famous enough to have her very own World Wide Web homepage: www.lizzie-borden.com and she is part of the Welcome to the City page: *What do Lizzie Borden and Molten Metal Technology have in common? Both used cutting-edge technology to put the City of Fall River, Massachusetts, on the world map.*

At the Lizzie Borden Bed and Breakfast Museum, I can sleep in Lizzie's room or the one in which Abby, her stepmother, was murdered. For the faint hearted, there's The Bridget Sullivan Room, named for the Bordens' maid who discovered the bodies. Those who need reassurance from the law can nap with pictures of the family attorney in the Andrew Jennings Room or the district attorney in Hosea Knowlton's Room. All this and the Bordens' last meal of eggs, sausages, home fries, johnny cakes, cornbread and bananas with mutton broth for $219 a night. Plus, there are sugar cookies shaped like axes for the ride home. Lights flicker, video equipment turns on then off, cameras work when they shouldn't and don't work when they should.

This Greek Revival house is O. J. Simpson in a white Bronco on the San Diego Freeway. No Cinderella fabrication from Disney, it's the actual site of two murders. This New England industrial town of brick fortresses with empty windows to thread is no set from Universal. Once the largest manufacturer of printed cotton in the world, Fall River's pulse was first arrhythmic then gone along with noise of machines roaring in American Print Works that sucked up street conversation, caused children to drop balls and clap hands over their ears. Workers leaning for February breath out of fourth story windows might have been horses poking their heads out of stalls. No escape from textile dust, women kept lace curtains white as they blew in and out of unscreened houses. No way to block the sharp smell marching in front of men coming through the door, hands could not erase the residue of days staining work clothes by scrubbing with lye soap or salt. Stench of Troy Cotton and Woolen Manufactory is gone just as Stafford Mills is drained of men and women so tired they groaned getting into bed like a hull bruising against barnacles, their last breath a sucking like the Atlantic as it ebbed from the docks. Lives narrowing to a crust of ice funneling the road, all that's left of Durfee Mills are stacks of letters bundled with rubber bands, pages brittle as insect wings, that I find when I go to the Historical Society to do research. More exciting is the yellowed trial tag reading *Mr. Borden's stomach*. Yes, I'm disappointed red gobs on the tag turn out to be sealing wax, but spots on Abby Borden's bedspread and her pillowcase are real enough like the skulls, or what's left of them.

What I admire most about Lizzie is her creativity. Following like fish in a school, her stories all started with she hadn't heard a thing. When the murders occurred: she had been out in the barn eating pears when her stepmother went up to the guest room to change the linens; she was out in the barn looking for fishing sinkers; she was in the dining room ironing and folding handkerchiefs while her father was murdered catnapping in the sitting room ten feet away. Surprisingly little blood was on her dress but she burned it the following day in the kitchen stove. Maybe she wasn't getting rid of evidence but was just too tired to wash, was low on coal or so sensitive she couldn't bear to wear her father's blood.

Arrested, no prayer or rosary snaked around her wrist. There was no way she would confess — like granite, conceded nothing. The judge was no pulley and winch, coaxing Lizzie, convincing her inch by inch with talk of ropes. After a thirteen-day trial, she was acquitted in one hour. Maybe the jury wanted to believe her story, couldn't believe a daughter of a prosperous furniture merchant would commit such a crime. It's also possible, they'd never left Taunton River's banks, never seen cabins perched in hollows of narrow valleys wallpapered in green cedar of the Appalachians. It is a real pity that just one juror did not visit forested ridges of Harlan County, Kentucky, to watch my mother give our hog a sharp blow on the head with an axe while her sister stuck him in the jugular about three inches back from the left jawbone. Then, everyone, understanding the power hidden in a woman's arm, the accuracy of her aim, would have realized Lizzie possessed the will, the strength to raise an axe twenty-nine times.

A boat built with dry wood that takes up water and never gives it up, Lizzie showed no sign of grief to melt neighboring hearts like snow.

Shunned for life, never weighted by remorse like a dory built with
green wood so water won't seep in, she was fit enough to row alone
out into the ocean. Enduring until 1927, buried in her family plot,
Lizzie Borden continues to live like smoke rising unlike other women
of Fall River whose days are condensed on a gravestone and chiseled
with a man's last name. Cleaning, cooking and canning died with their
good deeds. Nothing of life preserved the hard way is displayed like a
wasp in amber or hair locketed in gold for women who didn't know
Latin names of plants but believed in the miracle of loaves and fishes.
No bottled bathwater is sold like a saint's tears for those who made
chicken and dumplings materialize in their hands. Tourists like me
come to Oak Grove Cemetery to lean on an axe handle not to count
how many years were spent weeding gardens with no hope of bloom
or to finger the names resting on pain of childbirth, lasting like a laurel,
like a rose.

PRIME TIME BARRY SILESKY

"How do you comport yourself with Jack the Ripper?"
— Gerald Burns

Did you hear it? I have to look back: one eye, the gleam in black
spilling out of its frame: a museum piece? Safe that way, but then
he's in the mirror, drinking my brandy, and all I can think is sleep. It
comes finally, but in patches; we've assembled the axe, the hammer,
the knife next to the bed, as the knock rattles the window. Carefully,
with aching slowness, one step on the carpet, another, tense in the
still hall: anything but to wake that breathing. The train hums in the
distance, it must be coming, but never soon enough. The whimper
spills under the door, the stomach turns in the throat. Armor forged,
mask donned, the years ravel out the window. I promise help, wish him
luck, buy him a drink: have the tv, stereo. Here, let me help you with
those packages, really, we all want the same thing. Except, of course, he
doesn't. Leering out of the stairwell, it's another language completely.
Put him away quick. The cops don't believe me and the prisons are
bursting. Why else is he here? Please, a last drink to deaden the skin.

THIS IS HOW IT COMES R. T. SMITH

— Opelika, Alabama

I was just setting on the porch
this morning in my undershirt
rocking and having a smoke before breakfast

when he come over the cow fence.
I never seen him before
with a straight razor in the hand,
a wild look on his demon face.

Just rush up the steps and flick out
here across my nose
and here on my wrist like he was trying
to kill myself for me,

then run back and jump the fence
with a scream like that redbone bitch
bit into the wasp nest last June.
Left me setting here bleeding
and run off in the direction of the sun.

Like I say, I never
seen him or any such in my life before.
He just leave me here bleeding
on my coveralls, and Mayelle calls me,
"The eggs is ready," before I can say
that something just ain't right.

SUBURBAN CRIMES III DAVID STARKEY

Battery: A woman punched her husband in the face several times because he
wasn't paying attention to her at 8:40 A.M. Tuesday, March 3, at their home on
the 2000 block of Fox Pointe Drive.
  — from the Aurora, Illinois, police blotter

Because a wife can be expected to endure
the familiar hulk of her husband
for just so long. The way his affections
have dimmed, the years he's spent
sitting sentinel before hockey games
and golf tournaments, these are ordeals
like those faced by ascetics and shaman;
anthropologists should recognize
this fact. In time, skin wrinkles:
science has already proven that.
Faith protracted flickers down to ash,
and when it's wholly burnt a woman
will stand at the door observing
her man's stark calm with growing
rage, until she stops needing to squint.
It's all clear. Then, while he mumbles
his day's agenda, she will cock
her arm and land her fist against his chin.
It will feel good, like pounding meat
with a wooden mallet or chopping
raw carrots with a very sharp knife.
Yet even this will not be enough.
He may go on talking, or his silence
alone may prompt one more blow,
and perhaps another. The moment
afterwards is always somber.
How a man reacts to such a crisis
tells everything about his nerve.
How a woman acts tells more.

GRANITE JAW MARK TAKSA

The dormitory is full of radios fighting to be loud.
The bully spits into the sink I use when he naps.

The price of brushing my teeth, he shouts,
is knifing a buddy. I am a rabbit in a fox cage.

I steal a knife from the chow hall,
push it into the throat selling the sink.

The waif mate is draining life. I rip
my undershirt, push light into the cut,

push fear to the back of my iron eyes, tighten my jaw
to granite. Out of a dusty gullet, I am promising.

MY GRANDMOTHER'S BIRTHDAY SUSAN THOMAS

My grandmother goes to visit a friend
in the projects on Ninth Avenue.
She is ninety years old today.
She wears a mink coat, brown suede pumps,
cut-garnet earrings and garnet broach.
In the elevator a young man
pushes her to the ground.
He puts his high-heeled boot to her neck.
My grandmother lies still.
Then she starts to scream.
She pushes his foot off her neck
and jumps up with the strength
she had sixty years ago.
The young man runs out of the elevator
and down six flights of stairs.
My grandmother is still screaming.
The garnets shake on her ears and her bosom.

MODERN LOVE ANN TOWNSEND

The rain streams past the gutters, overflowing
    a drain clogged with leaves. From inside
the sound is cool and precise, and though
    the door lies open and the light
spills out, the kitchen keeps its warmth.
    The refrigerator hums, the girl works on
beneath the pools of light, and the man
    outside her window sees her pull
on a cigarette; his eyes follow
    the orange-bright tip; he flicks water
from his eyes and wonders what to do next,
    how to proceed, whether to use the knife
or his hands to open the latched screen door.
    He has never been so wet.

She studies the list on the table, decorum
    of crossed-out items — the few that remain.
The rain slows, and the last crickets begin
    a feeble song from the pond next door.
So far away, each thinks. He watches her mouth open
    in concentration. He must make her
hear him as he meant to be heard:
    what they have done has not been wrong.
His hands know their way past the buttons of her dress.
    She lifts her eyes to the window and catches
sight of her own likeness in the glass.
    She can never stop herself: smiling
at the ghost reflection before her.
    He believes she is looking at him.

> *. . . and it seem as though I could*
> *see ny heart before ny eyes, turning*
> *dark black with Hate of Rages, or*
> *harhequinade, stripped from that munner*
> *life leaving only naked being-Hate.*
> *— Charles Starkweather*

On the Great Plains in March
the wind blows for days.
Gutter pipes vibrate, shingles flap;
things begin to come loose.
Once they found old Miss Purdy
wandering at midnight on U.S. 40,
her nightgown billowing
over her spindly, blue-gray thighs.
It took three deputies to hold her down
till the doctor arrived.

On the Great Plains in March
the dry elm scrapes
at an upstairs window,
dust devils swirl and disperse
across the wide, empty fields,
and a pistol shot sounds
no louder than a screen door
slapping on a porch.

A BOY EXPLODED ON THE CORNER TODAY SETH TUCKER

In front of everybody
his face
a piece of parchment
bitter and acid stained
      And nobody sees him
      this boy,
      this columbite
      this swirling mineral
      was going Nuclear
            No brave last
            words
            no Quixotian
            murmur
            just
            BOOM
                  I wanted to hide
                  Under a dove-girl
                  see
                  my
                  hands.
                        Feel the nerve of it all
                        Can't you just hear what
                        Your mother would say?
Just another nigger blowing up
Just another chemistry experiment
Gone awry.
      Who is angry
      Who misses those
      Outlandish spectacles
      But the goofy parents
            To us, he is only swirling debris
                  To them   He is pamphlets and circumstance
                  He was our future
                        Attached to a gun.

KNIFE GLORIA VANDO

She was old. She lived alone in a small house
two blocks away. When they found her, days after,
she had been stabbed seventeen times — as if
a host of assassins had struck an empress down.
She might have even looked up briefly
before the final cut, spurting blood and
an imperious last line or two. Perhaps not.
Perhaps the first wound had done the trick —
the rest sport for the mad or wicked. A handyman
lived nearby. He worked odd jobs while leading
a secret life with his neighbor's Anglo wife,
who would sneak him in when her husband
and her son were out. No one questioned
Sanchez about the old lady. He traveled alone.
This was a gang job. One day while walking past
a vacant lot close by the boy spots a shiny
object winking at him through layers of rust
like a cheap sequin — summoning him to stoop
down, swoop it up, later to brandish it
with pride before his mother's sucked
astonishment. Give it here, she says.
The name on the crudely carved handle is clear,
letters printed in black Magic Marker — but
are they clearly the handyman's? Sanchez
is a common name. She knows he doesn't stand
a chance if he stands trial. Knows they'll find
guilt hidden like stacks of money unexplained
beneath the floorboards of his mind. She knows
Texas. Knows how stuff gets planted when you're
a Mexican without an alibi and they need
a solution. And most of all she knows, knows
as she digs the tiny grave for the homemade knife,
knows as she pats the soil over it and sows
the seeds of justice, knows as she pours
a 50-50 mixture of water and fish emulsion
over it to make the seeds grow, knows, damn it,
she just knows that he is guilty as hell.

ON REPORTING THE MURDER
OF A YOUNG PROSTITUTE JUDITH VOLLMER

I stood over her,
thought: *Draw me something,*
show me what you look at
when you're dreaming —
cops elbowed past me adjusting lights, tape,
markers. The air was still thick with her
cologne, and her body covered except for her face
& lovely hair, and I was useless.
She made a bargain with herself & somebody
else in an airport motel while
jet trails made their lines above our heads.
I phoned my editor and tried
my slender theories: planned hit
or courier fuckup.
Who was she and what story could I tell,
I was so young myself,
first writing job
in a newsroom high off the street
above the yellow rivers & everything
about the city changing.
One of the last kids
to work the Edison Hotel's mini-
coke & skintrade. Worked
hard. Paid envelopes of cash.
She was 24, a size 4 or 6.
Beautiful nails. Beside her sat
a cheap leather case, like
art students carry.
I believed deBeauvoir:
The worst a woman can do
is to exchange her body for capital.

As I remember her
she looked like many of my students do now,
dressed for class as for the clubs.
She loves stones as much as they do.
Engagement rings their men
save for. The size and heft of a love.
Delicate enameled friendship

rings from their girlfriends.
Gaudy class rings
paid for by aunts
or godmothers. Yesterday
a student I barely know
wept in the parking lot:
"I can't remember who all I slept with last night."
She went to a party
of five partners & five rounds.
She remembers that much.
She's 20, pretty, mostly unhappy.
I wonder why she's in school.
I'm tired of chalk outlines,
tired of blind sympathy.
I offer her a sip of my Pepsi
& half of my sandwich.
To her I'm blind.

DEMONSTRATION: WOMEN'S HOUSE
OF DETENTION, 1965 MICHAEL WATERS

demolished 1973–74
in memoriam JL
d. 1980

Blood-inked political leaflets pelted Village streets,
a revamped Biblical plague,
the stringed, sodden, menses-red confetti of the damned
delivered upon tourists
thronging the annual sidewalk art exhibition,
unshaven sunglass'd Sunday
bohemians sporting Bermuda shorts and sandals,
sidestepping spontaneous
abstract splatters, the city's interactive canvas,
as blasphemous breezes arced
Sixth Avenue, the cries of revolutionary
angels celebrating ruin
as the quickening, laval ash smudged our doomed island.
I stared up at barred windows
as flame-licked hands emerged to launch sleek kamikaze
Paracletes, fourteen stories
suffused with curses and filth and rancorous laughter.
"Don't listen!" warned my mother
as we navigated Manhattan's hewn passages,
fleeing into a bookshop
off MacDougal — refuge from the clotted tongues of rain —
where Mother purchased for me
a slender volume of hip, nonsensical fables
whose author, the "smart" Beatle,
would be gunned down uptown from the siren-spooked wreckage,
the lascivious ghost-site
of stumped adolescence, the helter-skelter, holy,
fallen
      Women's House of D.

KILLING THE ANIMALS CHARLES HARPER WEBB

I shot a kit fox, a tapir, and an ibex.
I couldn't read the names, but I remembered
from the zoo back home. I was pissed
not to get a lion or giraffe or elephant,
but after I gut-shot the ibex, and watched it
thrash on the ground, bleating like a sheep
while I wasted four more rounds to shut it up,
I didn't envy anyone the elephant.

When I was 10, I shot a rabbit with a bow.
My arrow pinned together its back feet,
like Oedipus left on the mountain.
But no pitying shepherd saved it.
Br'er Rabbit ragged toward his burrow,
screaming, "Eee! Eee! Eee!"
Who would have guessed a rabbit
could make so much noise — or that dried
old women in shawls had so much blood?

If I get home, and some reporter asks me why,
what will I say? We fought so long . . .
We were so glad to be alive . . .

MEAT MICHELANGELO CHARLES HARPER WEBB

No matter how he scrubbed, every day
Dad dragged home bloody and stinking,
then cooked our dinner while Mom lay
around and drank. When he offered
to teach me his trade, how could I say, "No.
I want to study Art"? The only thing

that kept me sane for sixteen years
was knowing that, although Mom screamed
and stumbled nude around the house,
and sprawled — legs splayed like pliers —
when she passed out, Dad cared for me.
So I learned to use his hooks and saws

and knives. The first week, I threw up
twice a day; then I could view a carcass
without shuddering. Soon I could slit it open,
gut it, quarter it, divide delicacies
from dog food with style. "Meat
Michelangelo," my friends called me.

I stopped dreaming of the Pieta,
and Naked Maja, and odalisques light-years
removed from Mom. I joked about
"The Burgers of Calais," and dreamed
of steaks and chuckroasts, breasts
of chicken, legs of lamb in cellophane

whizzing around my head,
or falling on me from the sky,
knocking me down and burying me
under cold, bloody, quivering meat.
When, at a bus stop, a girl like a death-
angel, all in black, asked for a ride,

I felt the steel chisel of Fate.
She had nowhere to spend the night,
so I took her to my room,
and cooked two T-bones. When I tried
to kiss her, and she asked me
for "a little nip first," I knew what to do.

It's fifty years since Betty Bersinger,
pushing her baby in a stroller,
found my work on Norton Avenue.
I'd halved the girl — Dahlia — for ease
of carrying, and drained her blood
to make her marble-white.

I sliced off a few choice bits
where they'd be noticed, and arranged her
carefully as any dancer by Degas.
Then, like Michelangelo brushing
the last dust off David, I stepped away,
and gave her to the world.

MAD MAN STEVE WILSON

What ocean is waveless?
— Malay proverb

An upper arm rested on the stove, sweating
with grease, and downstairs in the basement
a woman slumped asleep against the water heater,
her face a puffy ball of blue dough.

"It was that wall," he said. "That wall
I couldn't get over. With blue morning glories, the rain
of vines down the stones, the smell of cold bread.
That wall. A mile of cells nestling

along the forehead." One woman
told how he'd tied her to the fireplace,
Zero Mostel chuckling from the phono,
and traced the curves of her breasts

with a glowing coal, making a path — swirling and smoking —
from here to there. From him to her.
"We find our way. A bit of rope.
A field of stones. The round and weighted call of owls.

Left in the dark, we make our own light."

LUCKY SMILE MICHELE WOLF

Yielding cell from celluloid, a script for two
Refined in the mind's crevasse, Hinckley
Had fixed on that actress, her grin
In the dark — the girl he had needed to impress.
He had wanted her flowery scent on his
Pillow, the small of her back against
His hand. "Her lucky smile," he revealed
In confinement, that was the feature he liked
The best. And this young woman, a freshman
In college, who had witnessed the same scene
As we had, on the screen that we live with,
That window that brings in the world
Upon waves we can't see in the sky, saw
The president shot, shoved into the limo,
The shooter seized, the head on the pavement
Leaking, Brady flat, sunk in a puddle
Of blood, and learned, so much sooner than
Most of us, just what a bullet is, the way it can
Lodge right behind the eyes, color all that one sees,
Leave a metallic remnant of blood lingering
On the tongue, a flavor it seems one will never
Be rid of. She uses her smile now to show
How the wounded stand, how blood can be mopped,
How to bandage, each lesson in character
So we carry a heartbeat heard
As we make our way out of the theater,
Blinking at the light, at a face
That we know, at an onslaught of others
That surely we'll never know,
At the weight of the roles
We must play, almost larger than life.

SURVIVALIST CAROLYNE WRIGHT

The rifle's beside you like a lover
when I crawl into bed. The barrel
gleams in the dark, an acceptable
emotion. Boxes of ammo shells
by the nightstand are unconditional
terms for love. You say

your aim's not calculated,
not a bargain struck with a father
training his misaligned sights
on you, cocking the hammer
of his numbered days,

but your personal myth — the basement
stocked with survival rations
for a world you swear
you're not a child of.
Every catalogue you open
subtracts early death
like a row of bull's-eyes
from its discount price.

I flip the light switch on.
Your eyes blink dreams back
for the showdown: a Socrates
hated unto hemlock, a Peter
crucified head-down for love. Already

I am one of the survivors.

NOTES ON CONTRIBUTORS

KIM ADDONIZIO is the author of three poetry collections from BOA Editions, the most recent of which is *Tell Me*. She also coauthored, with Dorianne Laux, *The Poet's Companion: A Guide to the Pleasures of Writing Poetry*. A book of her stories, *In the Box Called Pleasure*, was published in 1999. She lives in San Francisco.

LIZ AHL's poems have appeared in such journals as *American Voice, Sundog, Southern Poetry Review*, and *Ascent*. She teaches and writes in Lincoln, Nebraska, where she also serves as an editorial assistant at *Prairie Schooner*.

SANDRA ALCOSSER grew up in Indiana, received a B.A. from Purdue University, and earned an M.F.A. from the University of Montana, where she studied with Richard Hugo. She is the author of *Except by Nature*, which received the 1998 James Laughlin Award from the Academy of American Poets and was selected by Eamon Grennan for the 1997 National Poetry Series, and *A Fish to Feed All Hunger*, which was selected by James Tate to be the Associated Writing Programs Award Series winner in poetry. Her poems have appeared in *Black Warrior Review*, the *New Yorker*, the *Paris Review*, *Ploughshares, Poetry*, and the *Yale Review*. Alcosser is currently a professor of poetry, fiction, and feminist poetics at San Diego State University and has taught at the University of Michigan, the University of Montana, and Louisiana State University.

SHERMAN ALEXIE is a Spokane–Coeur d'Alene Indian from Wellpinit, Washington, on the Spokane Indian reservation. In 1992, Alexie received an NEA Poetry Fellowship. In 1998 and 1999, Alexie won the New York Heavyweight Championship Poetry Bout at the Taos Poetry Circus. Alexie's books of poetry include *Old Shirts & New Skins, First Indian on the Moon*, and *The Summer of Black Widows*. His most recent special edition chapbook is *The Man Who Loves Salmon*. Alexie is currently working on a new collection of short stories, a new collection of poetry, and the screenplay adaptation for *Reservation Blues*, which he will also direct and coproduce.

WILLIAM BAER is the author of *The Unfortunates*, which received the 1997 T. S. Eliot Award. He is also the editor of interviews with Derek Walcott, *Conversations with Derek Walcott*. His work has appeared in *Poetry, Ploughshares, Kenyon Review, Hudson Review*, and other literary journals.

DAVID BAKER is the author of seven books, most recently *Heresy and the Ideal: On Contemporary Poetry* (criticism, 2000) and *The Truth about Small Towns* (poems, 1998). His work has appeared in many magazines, such as the *Atlantic*, the *Nation*, the *New Yorker*, and

Poetry, and he has won awards and fellowships from the NEA, Society of Midland Authors, Poetry Society of America, and others. Baker is professor of English at Denison University and poetry editor of *Kenyon Review*.

BARRY BALLARD, of Burleson, Texas, has been published in *American Literary Review* and *Midwest Quarterly*. He recently won poetry awards from Snail's Pace Press and the University of Alaska.

JIM BARNES was born in Summerfield, Oklahoma, and is of Choctaw-Welsh descent. In the 1950s, after high school, he migrated to Oregon where he worked for ten years as a lumberjack. Later, he earned an M.A. and Ph.D. at the University of Arkansas. He was awarded an NEA Fellowship in 1978, a Rockefeller Foundation Bellagio Residency Fellowship in 1990, and a Fulbright Fellowship in 1994. He is presently writer-in-residence and professor of comparative literature at Truman State University, where he also edits *Chariton Review*.

EDWARD BARTÓK-BARATTA, a survivor of childhood abuse and trauma, grew up in Jersey City, New Jersey, and is the eighth of nine children. Following the murder of his brother on New York's Bowery, he worked for eight years with people who are homeless in Boston's Combat Zone. He is the founder of Fridays Are for Prisoners, an awareness-raising group that uses fasting and voluntary isolation to bring attention to the crisis in U.S. prisons, where more than 2 million Americans are housed. Bartók-Baratta's poems have appeared in *Denver Quarterly*, *Verse*, *Harvard Review*, *Virginia Quarterly Review*, and *Seneca Review*.

ELLEN BASS has a new book of poetry forthcoming in 2002. Her awards include the Elliston Book Award and *Nimrod*/Hardman's Pablo Neruda Prize. She is also coauthor of *The Courage to Heal* and worked for many years with survivors of child sexual abuse. Presently, she teaches creative writing in Santa Cruz, California.

JILL BIALOSKY is the author of *The End of Desire*, and coauthor of the anthology *Wanting a Child*. She is a vice-president and senior editor at W. W. Norton & Company and lives in New York City.

WENDY BISHOP teaches rhetoric, composition, and creative writing at Florida State University. She has published poems and stories in *American Poetry Review*, *Yale Review*, *Western Humanities Review*, as well as *Cream City Review*, and is the author of the textbook *Thirteen Ways of Looking for a Poem: A Guide to Writing Poetry*.

BRUCE BOND's books of poetry include *Independence Days* (R. Gross Award), *The Anteroom of Paradise* (Colladay Award), and most recently *Radiography* (Natalie Ornish Award). Presently he is director of creative writing at the University of North Texas and poetry editor for the *American Literary Review*.

JOHN BRADLEY is the editor of the anthologies *Atomic Ghost: Poets Respond to the Nuclear Age* and *Learning to Glow: A Nuclear Reader*. His poetry has appeared in *Caliban, Ironwood, Key Satch(el), Poetry East, The Prose Poem: An International Journal*, and other journals. His book of poems *Love-In-Idleness: The Poetry of Roberto Zingarello* won the Washington Prize, and he was the recipient of an NEA Fellowship. He teaches writing at Northern Illinois University and lives in DeKalb with his wife, Jana.

SEAN BRENDAN-BROWN currently works as a photographer for the insurance commissioner's Investigation Division in Washington. He received an M.F.A. from the Iowa Writers' Workshop and was awarded an NEA grant in 1997. His poems have appeared in *Notre Dame Review, Clackamas Literary Review, Texas Review*, and *Green Mountains Review*, among other literary journals. He has two chapbooks, *No Stopping Anytime* and *Monarch of Hatred*.

GAYLORD BREWER is an associate professor at Middle Tennessee State University, where he founded and edits *Poems & Plays*. His publications include *David Mamet and Film, Charles Bukowski*, and two collections of poems, *Presently a Beast* and *Devilfish*.

MICHAEL BUGEJA is on the advisory board of *Writer's Digest*, former honorary chair of the National Federation of State Poetry Societies, and special assistant to the president at Ohio University, where he also teaches writing and ethics. His poems have appeared in *Harper's, Poetry, Georgia Review, Kenyon Review, New England Review, Sewanee Review*, and many others. His latest collections are *Millennium's End* and *Talk*.

BRIGITTE BYRD was born in France and emigrated to the United States ten years ago. She lives in Tallahassee, Florida, where she pursues her doctoral studies in the creative writing program at Florida State University.

MARCUS CAFAGÑA's first book, *The Broken World*, was a National Poetry Series selection in 1996. His second book, *Roman Fever*, was published in 2001. His poems have appeared in journals and anthologies such as *American Poetry Review, Ploughshares, Poetry, Southern Review, Threepenny Review, TriQuarterly, Witness*, and *The Beacon Best of 1999: Creative Writing by Women and Men of All Colors*. He teaches in the creative writing program at Southwest Missouri State University.

RICK CAMPBELL is the director of Anhinga Press and the Anhinga Prize for Poetry and teaches English at Florida A&M University in Tallahassee. He has published work in many literary journals, including *Georgia Review*, *Missouri Review*, *Southern Poetry Review*, *Puerto Del Sol*, *Poet Lore*, *Chattahoochee Review*, *Prairie Schooner*, and *Tar River Poetry Review*. He has published two chapbooks, *Driving to Wyoming* and *The Breathers at St. Marks*. He has won an NEA Fellowship in Poetry and two poetry fellowships from the Florida Arts Council. He lives with his wife and daughter in Gadsden County.

SANDRA CASTILLO was born in Havana, Cuba, where she spent the first eight years of her life. She and her family were among the last Cubans to leave the island during the Johnson administration's Freedom Flights. Her poetry has appeared in various anthologies, including *North of Wakulla — An Anthology of Florida Poets*, *Paper Dance: An Anthology of Latino Poets*, *A Century of Cuban Writers in Florida*, and *Cool Salsa: On Growing Up Latino in the U.S.* A senior associate professor, she teaches at Miami Dade Community College in Miami, Florida. She recently completed a second poetry manuscript entitled *My Father Sings to My Embarrassment*.

LISA D. CHAVEZ received a B.A. from the University of Alaska, Fairbanks, and an M.F.A. from Arizona State University. Her poetry, creative nonfiction, and short stories have appeared in numerous literary magazines, and her first collection of poetry, *Destruction Bay*, appeared in 1998.

MAXINE CHERNOFF is the author of five books of poetry and five books of fiction. She is professor of creative writing at San Francisco State University and editor with Paul Hoover of the journal *New American Writing*. She has read from her work in Australia, Belgium, Germany, England, and Scotland.

PAUL CHRISTENSEN lives part of the year in southern France, where he contributes articles on French life and travel to *France Today* and other magazines. He is author of many books, including *Minding the Underworld* and *Charles Olson: Call Him Ishmael*. He has received an NEA Poetry Fellowship and a Fulbright Senior Lectureship, among other honors. He teaches modern literature and writing at Texas A&M University.

DAVID CITINO is professor of English and creative writing at Ohio State University. He is the author of ten collections of poetry, including *The Book of Appassionata: Collected Poems* and *Broken Symmetry*, which was named a Notable Book of 1997 by the National Book Critics Circle. He writes on poetry for the *Columbus Dispatch* and has a book of prose, *The Eye of the Poet*, forthcoming.

JEFFREY CLAPP grew up on a dairy farm in southern New Hampshire. He graduated from the University of New Hampshire where he won the Daniel Morin Poetry prize. He then worked as a laborer and housepainter for a few years before returning to the university as a student in the graduate writing program. He currently is a member of the English department at Dutchess Community College, Poughkeepsie, New York. His stories and poems have appeared in a number of journals and magazines, including one story that was nominated for a Pushcart and another that was winner of the Indiana Fiction Prize.

MICHAEL COLLIER was born in 1953 in Phoenix, Arizona, where he had most of his education, including graduate school at the University of Arizona. Since 1981, he has lived on the East Coast where he teaches at the University of Maryland. He has published four books of poetry, including *The Neighbor* and *The Ledge*. Since 1995, he has served as the director of the Bread Loaf Writers' Conference.

MARTHA COLLINS is the author of four volumes of poetry, the latest of which, *Some Things Words Can Do*, was published in 1998. She has also cotranslated and published with the author *The Women Carry River Water* (1997), a volume of Vietnamese poems by Nguyen Quang Thieu. She is the Pauline Delaney Professor of Creative Writing at Oberlin College where she also serves as an editor of *Field*.

NICOLE COOLEY grew up in New Orleans, Louisiana. She received a B.A. from Brown University, an M.F.A. from the Iowa Writers' Workshop, and a Ph.D. from Emory University. She is the author of *Resurrection*, which was chosen by Cynthia MacDonald for the 1995 Walt Whitman Award. Her poems have appeared in *Poetry*, *Field*, *Poetry Northwest*, *Ploughshares*, and the *Nation*. She received a "Discovery"/*The Nation* award for her poetry in 1994 and in 1996 received a fiction grant from the NEA. She taught at Bucknell University before accepting a position to teach creative writing at Queens College-CUNY. In 1998, her novel *Judy Garland, Ginger Love* was published. Cooley currently lives in New York City and is working on a book of poetry about the Salem witch trials of 1692, titled *The Afflicted Girls*.

PETER COOLEY was born in Detroit and grew up there and in the suburbs of the city. A graduate of Shimer College, the University of Chicago, and the University of Iowa, where he was a student in the Writers' Workshop and received a Ph.D., he is currently professor of English at Tulane University in New Orleans teaching creative writing. Married and the father of three children, he has published six books of poetry: *The Company of Strangers*, *The Room Where the Summer Ends*, *Nightseasons*, *The Van Gogh Notebook*, *The Astonished Hours*, and *Sacred Conversations*. Since 1970, he has been the poetry editor for *North American Review*.

MARY CROW, the poet laureate of Colorado, is the author of four books of poetry and three books of translation. She is currently finishing a new collection of poetry, *Islands*, as well as a book of translations, *Homesickness: Selected Poems of Enrique Lihn*. She has won a number of prizes including a poetry fellowship from the NEA, a creative writing award from the Fulbright Commission, a Colorado Book Award, and a translation award from the Translation Center of Columbia University. She teaches creative writing at Colorado State University.

ROBERT DANA's most recent books of poetry are *Summer* and *Hello, Stranger*. He also edited *A Community of Writers: Paul Engle and the Iowa Writers' Workshop*. Dana graduated in 1954 from the Iowa Writers' Workshop where he studied with Robert Lowell and John Berryman. He has served as a distinguished visiting writer at universities in the U.S. and abroad, and after forty years of teaching at Cornell College he retired in 1994 as professor of English and poet-in-residence. His work was awarded NEA fellowships in 1985 and 1993, the Delmore Schwartz Memorial Poetry Award in 1989, and a Pushcart Prize in 1996.

JIM DANIELS was born in Detroit in 1956. His most recent book of poems is *Blue Jesus*. He is also the author of *No Pets*, a collection of stories, and wrote the screenplay for *No Pets*, a 1994 independent feature film. He edited *Letters to America: Contemporary American Poetry on Race* and coedited *American Poetry: The Next Generation*.

CHRISTOPHER DAVIS was born in 1960 in Whittier, California, received a B.A. in English from Syracuse University and an M.F.A. from the Iowa Writers' Workshop and is currently associate professor of creative writing at the University of North Carolina, Charlotte. His first collection of poetry, *The Tyrant of the Past and the Slave of the Future*, won the 1988 Associated Writing Programs award and his second, *The Patriot,* won the 1998 University of Georgia Press Contemporary Poetry Series competition. His third collection will be called *A History of the Only War*, and poems included in the manuscript have appeared in many journals, including *Harvard Review*, *Denver Quarterly*, *Boston Book Review*, *Pequod*, *Massachusetts Review*, *Volt*, and *Fence*.

ALISON HAWTHORNE DEMING is the great-great-granddaughter of Nathaniel Hawthorne. Her collection of poetry, *Science and Other Poems*, was selected by Gerald Stern for the Walt Whitman Award of the Academy of American Poets. Deming is the director of the Poetry Center at the University of Arizona and has been awarded numerous fellowships, including NEA and Stegner fellowships. Her poems and essays have appeared in many publications. She lives in Tucson, Arizona.

TOI DERRICOTTE has published four books of poetry. Her latest book, *Tender*, received the Paterson Poetry Prize for 1998. Her memoir, *The Black Notebooks*, published in 1997, was chosen by the *New York Times* to be a notable book of the year. She is a professor of English at the University of Pittsburgh and has taught in the graduate creative writing programs at New York University, George Mason University, Old Dominion University, and Mills College. In 1999–2000 she was the Delta Sigma Theta Endowed Chair in Poetry at Xavier University. She is cofounder of Cave Canem, the historic workshop retreat for African American poets.

SEAN THOMAS DOUGHERTY was born in New York City and raised in a politically radical interracial family, with a mother of Jewish/Okie descent and an African American stepfather, in Brooklyn, New York, Toledo, Ohio, and Manchester, New Hampshire. A former high school dropout, he's worked in factories, at a newspaper plant, a sawmill, and as a teacher. A widely hailed performance poet, he is the author of three full-length books: *The Body's Precarious Balance*; *Love Song of the Young Couple, the Dumb Job*, introduced by Patricia Smith; and *The Mercy of Sleep*, introduced by Christopher Buckley. He teaches at Syracuse University where he is completing a Ph.D. in cultural rhetoric and is a poet-in-the-schools along the East Coast.

DENISE DUHAMEL is an assistant professor of creative writing at Florida International University in Miami. She is the recipient of a New York Foundation for the Arts Fellowship, a Poets & Writers "Writers Exchange" award, *Prairie Schooner*'s Strousse Award, and a Ludwig Vogelstein Award in Poetry. She previously taught at New York City's West Side Y, Rutgers University, Bucknell University, the American University, and Lycoming College. Her work has been anthologized in such volumes as *American Poetry: Next Generation*, *New Young American Poets*, and the *Best American Poetry* (editions 2000, 1998, 1994, and 1993). She is married to poet Nick Carbo.

STUART DYBEK recently was a visiting writer at the Iowa Writers' Workshop. His poetry, fiction, and essays have appeared or are forthcoming in *Doubletake*, *Five Points*, *Harper's*, and *TriQuarterly*.

MARTÍN ESPADA, born in Brooklyn of Puerto Rican descent, has won two fellowships from the NEA, a Massachusetts Artists' Fellowship, a PEN/Revson Fellowship, and a Paterson Poetry Prize. In addition to writing poetry and university teaching, Espada has been a tenant lawyer in Chelsea, Massachusetts, a factory worker, and the desk

clerk on the night shift at a transient hotel. He also regularly
volunteers his time to work with disadvantaged children in cities
such as Holyoke, Springfield, and Hartford. His newest poetry
collection is *A Mayan Astronomer in Hell's Kitchen*.

SYBIL PITTMAN ESTESS was born in Mississippi. She received an
undergraduate degree from Baylor University and a Ph.D. from
Syracuse University. She is author of a book of poetry, *Seeing the
Desert Green*, and has coedited a book of criticism, *Elizabeth Bishop
and Her Art*. Estess has published poems in *Shenandoah*, *Paris
Review*, *New Republic*, *Western Humanities Review*, and *Southern
Poetry Review*. She currently lives in Houston and teaches writing
at Blinn College in Brenham, Texas.

STEVE FAY's collection of poems *what nature* was a finalist for the
annual poetry book award given by the Society of Midland Authors
and has been listed as recommended reading by *Orion*, a premier
venue for environmental writing. Fay divides his time between
South Beloit, Illinois, a suburb of Rockford, and a small acreage in
downstate Fulton County. He teaches at Beloit College.

REGINALD GIBBONS's most recent books of poems are *Sparrow:
New and Selected Poems*, which won the 1998 Balcones Poetry Prize,
and *Homage to Longshot O'Leary*. A paperback edition of his novel
Sweetbitter was issued in 1996, and his translation of Euripides'
Bakkhai is forthcoming. From 1981 till 1997 he was the editor of
TriQuarterly at Northwestern University where he is currently a
professor of English.

DIANE GLANCY teaches Native American Literature and Creative
Writing at Macalester College in St. Paul, Minnesota. She published
five books in 1999: *The Voice That Was in Travel*, *Fuller Man*, *The
Closets of Heaven*, *(Ado)ration*, and *Visit Teepee Towns*, *Native Writings
after the Detours*. A new collection of poems, *The Relief of America*, is
forthcoming. Glancy has an M.F.A. from the University of Iowa.

PATRICIA GOEDICKE has published twelve books of poetry, the most
recent of which is *As Earth Begins to End*. Other books include
Invisible Horses, *The Tongues We Speak*, *Paul Bunyan's Bearskin*, and
The Wind of Our Going. She grew up in New Hampshire, lived in
Ohio, and then spent twelve years in Mexico, following which she
returned to the U.S., first teaching at Sarah Lawrence College
and since then at the University of Montana, Missoula.

ALBERT GOLDBARTH has been publishing notable books of poetry
for over a quarter of a century, including *Heaven and Earth*, which
won the National Book Critics Circle Award, and his most recent
collection, *Troubled Lovers in History*. He is also the author of three
volumes of essays. He lives in Wichita, Kansas.

RAY GONZALEZ is the author of five books of poetry, including *The Heat of Arrivals*, and a book of essays, *Memory Fever: A Journey beyond El Paso del Norte*. He is the editor of numerous anthologies and received a 1993 Before Columbus Foundation American Book Award for Excellence in Editing. His most recent book of poetry is *Cabato Sentora*. He is professor of English at the University of Minnesota.

RIGOBERTO GONZÁLEZ is the author of *So Often the Pitcher Goes to Water until It Breaks*, a selection of the National Poetry Series. His writing has been featured in *American Poetry: Next Generation* and *Mama's Boy: Gay Men Write about Their Mothers* and has appeared in *Colorado Review*, *Chelsea*, and *Iowa Review*. A recipient of a John Simon Guggenheim Memorial Foundation Fellowship, he works as a bilingual literacy teacher in Brooklyn, New York.

BENJAMIN SCOTT GROSSBERG earned a Ph.D. in creative writing and literature from the University of Houston, where he completed an M.F.A. in 1996. His poems have appeared widely, in journals such as *Malahat Review*, *Paris Review*, and *Nimrod* and in the Alyson Publications Anthology, *Gents, Bad Boys and Barbarians*. His studies of literature may be found in the *Journal of Homosexuality* and *Studies in American Fiction*. He is currently completing his first book manuscript, *This Dream of Swimming the Hellespont*, and teaching literature and writing workshops in Houston, Texas.

LILACE MELLIN GUIGNARD has an M.F.A. from the University of California, Irvine, after which she returned to the southern Appalachians to kayak, write, and teach English and environmental seminars at an experiential high school. Her poems have appeared in *Sundog: The Southeast Review*, *Faultline*, *Asheville Poetry Review*, *Amaranth*, and others. She is currently studying literature and environment at the University of Nevada, Reno, and is working on a memoir, *Time to Plant Tears*.

LOLA HASKINS has published six books of poems, most recently *Extranjera* and *Desire Lines, New and Selected Poems*. She teaches at the University of Florida, Gainesville.

JUAN FELIPE HERRERA's recent books include *Border-Crosser with a Lamborghini Dream*, *Loteria Cards & Fortune Poems: The Book of Lives*, and *Crashboomlove*. He lives in Fresno, California, with his soul-partner, Margarita Luna Robles.

BOB HICOK's *Plus Shipping* was published in 1998. *The Legend of Light* won the 1995 Felix Pollak Prize and was an ALA Notable Book of the Year. An NEA Fellow for 1999, his poetry has appeared in *Best American Poetry* (1997 and 1999) and the Pushcart Prize 2000. He owns an automotive die design business.

CYNTHIA HOGUE has lived in nonviolent communities (Rekjavik, Iceland, and Copenhagen, Denmark) as well as urban American communities that see a fair amount of violence (Tucson and New Orleans). She is a trained mediator as well as teaching writer. She has published three collections of poetry, most recently *The Never Wife*, and a critical book on American women's poetry. She currently lives in Pennsylvania where she directs the Stadler Center for Poetry and teaches English at Bucknell University.

JANET HOLMES is author of *The Green Tuxedo* and *The Physicist at the Mall*. Her work has twice been chosen to appear in the *Best American Poetry* volumes and she has received the Pablo Neruda Prize as well as fellowships from the Bush Foundation, the McKnight Foundation, and the Minnesota State Arts Board. *The Green Tuxedo* was named *ForeWord* magazine's book of the year in poetry and won the 1999 Minnesota Book Award. Holmes lives in Boise, Idaho, and teaches full-time in the M.F.A. program for writers at Boise State University.

PAUL HOOVER is author of seven poetry collections, including *Totem and Shadow: New & Selected Poems*, *Viridian*, *The Novel: A Poem*, and *Idea*, which won the Carl Sandburg Award given by Friends of the Chicago Public Library. His poetry has appeared in *American Poetry Review*, *New Republic*, *Paris Review*, *Sulfur*, *Conjunctions*, *TriQuarterly*, and *Partisan Review*, among others. His work has also been included in five editions of the *Best American Poetry*. He is editor of a major anthology, *Postmodern American Poetry*, and with Maxine Chernoff also edits the literary magazine *New American Writing*.

AUSTIN HUMMELL was born in Mandarin, Florida, in 1963. His first book, *The Fugitive Kind*, won the Contemporary Poetry Series and was published in 1997. His poems also appear in the anthology *American Poetry: The Next Generation*. He holds a Ph.D. from the University of Missouri, Columbia, and is an assistant professor of English at the University of North Texas.

MARK JARMAN's latest collection of poetry, *Questions for Ecclesiastes*, won the Lenore Marshall Poetry Prize for 1998 and was a finalist for the 1997 National Book Critics Circle Award. He is coeditor of *Rebel Angels: 25 Poets of the New Formalism* and coauthor of *The Reaper Essays*. His book of essays, *The Secret of Poetry*, is forthcoming, as is his next collection of poetry, *Unholy Sonnets*. He teaches at Vanderbilt University.

LARRY WAYNE JOHNS is currently a Kingsbury Fellow in the Ph.D. program at Florida State University. He received a Reader's Choice

Award from *Prairie Schooner* and the first annual Frank O'Hara Award for his chapbook *An Invisible Veil between Us*.

PETER JOHNSON is founder and editor of *The Prose Poem: An International Journal*. He has published two books of prose poems, *Pretty Happy!* and *Love Poems for the Millennium*. His chapbook, *I'm a Man*, won Raincrow Press's 1997 Chapbook Fiction Contest. He received a creative writing fellowship in 1999 from the NEA.

ALLISON JOSEPH was born in London to Caribbean parents and grew up in Toronto, Canada, and the Bronx, New York. She was educated at Kenyon College and Indiana University. Currently, she lives in Carbondale, Illinois, where she teaches at Southern Illinois University. Her books of poems are *What Keeps Us Here*, *Soul Train*, and *In Every Seam*.

RODGER KAMENETZ is the author of *The Missing Jew: New and Selected Poems*, *Stuck: Poems Midlife*, as well as *Terra Infirma*, *Stalking Elijah*, and *The Jew in the Lotus*. In 1995, he created the first Louisiana Diaspora People's Conference at LSU where he teaches poetry and nonfiction writing and directs the Jewish Studies minor. His poems have been anthologized in all the major collections of Jewish American poetry in recent years.

JARRET KEENE teaches at Florida State University where he also serves as editor of *Sundog: The Southeast Review*. His stories, essays, and verse have appeared in *River Styx*, *Poetry Motel*, and *New England Review*.

DAVID KIRBY is W. Guy McKenzie Professor of English at Florida State University and is the author of four poetry collections, including *The House of Blue Light*. His poems and reviews have appeared in *Parnassus*, *Southern Review*, and *New Orleans Review*.

WILLIAM KLOEFKORN teaches and writes in Lincoln, Nebraska. He has authored more than a dozen collections of poetry, among them *Dragging Sand Creek for Minnows*, *Drinking the Tin Cup Dry*, *Covenants* (with Utah poet David Lee), and, most recently, *Treehouse: New & Selected Poems* and *Welcome to Carlos*. His memoir, *This Death by Drowning*, was published in the fall of 1997. He and his wife, Eloise, have four children and a pleasant assortment of grandchildren.

JEFF KNORR teaches writing and literature at Clackamas Community College in Oregon City, Oregon, where he also coedits the *Clackamas Literary Review*. His work has appeared in *Red Brick Review*, *Connecticut Review*, *Red Rock Review*, and *Oxford Magazine*, as well as others. His poems have also been anthologized by Black Buzzard Press, Native West Press, and Adrienne Lee Press. He was also nominated for a Pushcart Prize. His first collection of poems, *Standing Up to the Day*, was published in 1999.

MARILYN KRYSL lives and works in the U.S. She has also worked for Mother Teresa's Sisters of Charity at the Kalighat Home for the Destitute and Dying in Calcutta and for Peace Brigade International in Sri Lanka. Her poetry collection, *Warscape with Lovers*, won the Cleveland State Poetry Center Prize in 1996. Her most recent book is a short story collection, *How to Accommodate Men*.

DAVID LAZAR's work has appeared in the *Anchor Essay Annual: Best of 1998*, *Chelsea*, *Southwest Review*, *Denver Quarterly*, and other journals and magazines. He has four citations for Notable Essays of the Year from *Best American Essays* and his work is included in *Prose Poem: An International Journal*. He edited *Conversations with M. F. K. Fisher* and *Michael Powell: Interviews* and is a member of the creative writing faculty at Ohio University.

LAURENCE LIEBERMAN has published twelve books of poetry, including *Flight from the Mother Stone* and *The Regatta in the Skies: Selected Long Poems*. His poems and critical essays have appeared in most of the country's leading magazines, among them *Atlantic Monthly*, the *New Yorker*, *New Republic*, *American Poetry Review*, *Hudson Review*, *Partisan Review*, *Kenyon Review*, and *Sewanee Review*. Lieberman received a Jerome Shestack Prize from *American Poetry Review* for the title sequence from his book *The Mural of Wakeful Sleep* and was awarded an NEA Fellowship supporting his cycle of Caribbean poetry books in progress. He is currently professor of English at the University of Illinois, Champaign-Urbana, and poetry editor for University of Illinois Press.

TIMOTHY LIU's first book of poems, *Vox Angelica*, received the 1992 Norma Farber First Book Award from the Poetry Society of America. Two subsequent collections have been published, *Burnt Offerings* (1995) and *Say Goodnight* (1998). Widely published in such journals as *Grand Street*, the *Nation*, and *Paris Review*, Liu is also the editor of *Word of Mouth: An Anthology of Gay American Poetry*. He was the 1997 Holloway Lecturer at the University of California, Berkeley, and currently teaches at William Paterson University in New Jersey.

RACHEL LODEN's collection *Hotel Imperium* won the Contemporary Poetry Series competition in 1999. Her chapbook, *The Last Campaign*, won the Hudson Valley Writers' Center competition and her poems have appeared in *Paris Review*, *Antioch Review*, *New American Writing*, *Boulevard*, and *Best American Poetry 1995*. She lives in Palo Alto, California.

MONIFA LOVE is the author of the novel *Freedom in the Dismal* and *Provisions*, a volume of poetry published in 1989. She is the director of Free Zone Productions and teaches at Florida State University where she serves as the Ed Love Visiting Professor of Black Studies. She recently completed a second novel and a new collection of poetry. She is at work on *After the Rain: Life with an Extraordinary Man*.

JOANNE LOWERY's poems have appeared in many literary magazines, including *Columbia*, *Florida Review*, *Northwest Review*, *Seneca Review*, and *River Styx*. Her fourth collection, *Double Feature*, was published in 2000. She lives in northern Indiana.

JOHN LUNDBERG holds a B.A. from the College of William and Mary and is a candidate for an M.A. in creative writing at Florida State University. His poetry has recently appeared in *Quarterly West*, *Sycamore Review*, *Iconoclast*, and *Poetry*.

WALT McDONALD was an air force pilot, taught at the Air Force Academy, and is now director of creative writing at Texas Tech. He has published eighteen collections of poetry and fiction, including *Blessings the Body Gave*, *The Flying Dutchman*, *Counting Survivors*, *Night Landings*, and *After the Noise of Saigon*. Three books won awards from the National Cowboy Hall of Fame. More than 1,800 of his poems have been published in such journals as *Atlantic Monthly*, the *Nation*, *New York Review of Books*, *Paris Review*, *Poetry*, *Sewanee Review*, *Southern Review*, *Sundog: The Southeast Review*, and *TriQuarterly*.

CAMPBELL McGRATH is the author of three previous full-length collections: *Capitalism*, *American Noise*, and *Spring Comes to Chicago*. His recent awards include the Kingsley Tufts Prize, the Cohen Prize, a Guggenheim Fellowship, a Witter-Bynner Fellowship from the Library of Congress in association with the poet laureate, and a MacArthur Fellowship. McGrath teaches creative writing at Florida International University and lives in Miami Beach with his wife and two sons.

PETER MEINKE has published six collections, the most recent being *Zinc Fingers* (2000) and *Scars* (1996). His book *Liquid Paper: New & Selected Poems* (1991) is in its third printing. Among his awards are the Olivet Prize, the Paumanok Award, three prizes from the Poetry Society of America, two NEA fellowships in poetry, and the Flannery O'Connor Award for his short story collection, *The Piano Turner*. He retired from directing the writing workshop at Eckerd College in 1993 and since then has been writer-in-residence at the University of North Carolina, Greensboro, the University of

Hawai'i, Randolph-Macon Women's College, and other schools and universities. He lives in St. Petersburg, Florida.

DONALD MORRILL's poems and prose have appeared in numerous magazines, including *Georgia Review*, *Creative Nonfiction*, *Southern Review*, and *North American Review*. He is winner of the *Missouri Review* editors' prize for nonfiction and is the author of *A Stranger's Neighborhood*, a memoir, and *At the Bottom of the Sky*, a poetry collection that won the Mid-List First Series Award.

RICHARD NEWMAN's poetry and essays have recently appeared in *Black Dirt*, *Boulevard*, *Crab Orchard Review*, *Slant*, *Southern Humanities Review*, *Spoon River Poetry Review*, and others. He edits *River Styx* in St. Louis, Missouri.

AIMEE NEZHUKUMATATHIL was born in Chicago and received an M.F.A. from Ohio State University. She is the author of a chapbook, *Fishbone*, and her honors include a fellowship from the Wisconsin Institute for Creative Writing and an AWP Intro Award for creative nonfiction. Her essays and poems have appeared in *Beloit Poetry Journal*, *Chelsea*, *Crab Orchard Review*, *Mid-American Review*, and *Quarterly West*.

DEBRA NYSTROM teaches creative writing at the University of Virginia. Her first book, *A Quarter Turn*, was published in 1991. She was awarded a postgraduate Hoyns Fellowship from the University of Virginia and has received the James Boatwright Prize from *Shenandoah*, the Balch Prize from the *Virginia Quarterly Review*, and two poetry fellowships from the Virginia Commission for the Arts. "Regardless of the Final Score" is from a recently completed manuscript entitled *The Cliff Swallows*.

BILJANA D. OBRADOVIČ, originally from Yugoslavia, has a Ph.D. in English from the University of Nebraska. Her second bilingual collection of poems, *Le Riche Monde*, appeared in late 1999. She is an assistant professor of English at Xavier University and is a member of the Association of Writers of Serbia. Her newest project is a bilingual translation of five American and five Serbian poets.

ED OCHESTER's most recent books of poetry are *Cooking in Key West* (chapbook), *Snow White Horses: Selected Poems, 1973–1988*, and *The Land of Cockaigne*. He is the editor of the Pitt Poetry Series and the general editor of the Drue Heinz Literature Prize for short fiction and for many years was director of the writing program at the University of Pittsburgh. He currently teaches in the M.F.A. writing seminars at Bennington College.

WILLIAM OLSEN's third poetry collection, *Trouble Lights*, was published in 2001. His poetry has appeared in the anthologies *New American Poets of the Nineties* and *The Breadloaf Anthology of*

Contemporary American Poetry. He teaches at Western Michigan University and at the M.F.A. program in writing at Vermont College.

STEVE ORLEN teaches at the University of Arizona in Tucson and in the low-residency M.F.A. program at Warren Wilson College. His latest book of poems, *Kisses,* was published in 1997 and his poems have recently appeared in the *Harvard Review, TriQuarterly,* and the *Yale Review.*

DIXIE PARTRIDGE's poetry has appeared in *America, Borderlands, Commonweal, Georgia Review,* and the *Anthology of Magazine Verse/Yearbook of American Poetry, 1997.* Her essays have also appeared widely in national and regional journals.

ROBERT PHILLIPS's fifth collection of poetry, *Breakdown Lane,* has gone into its second printing. His sixth collection, *Spinach Days,* was issued in the spring of 2000. He is former director of the creative writing program and John and Rebecca Moores Scholar at the University of Houston. Phillips's prizes include an award in literature from the American Academy of Arts and Letters. Three of his books have been named a notable book of the year by the *New York Times Book Review.* He is poetry editor of *Texas Review* and a councilor of the Texas Institute of Letters.

STANLEY PLUMLY is a distinguished university professor at the University of Maryland. His new collection, *Now That My Father Lies Down beside Me: New & Selected Poems,* is forthcoming.

KEVIN PRUFER is the author of *Strange Wood,* which won the Winthrop Poetry Series. He is also editor of *The New Young American Poets* and *Pleiades: A Journal of New Writing.* His newest poems appear in *Southern Review, Prairie Schooner, Antioch Review, Boulevard,* and *TriQuarterly.*

WYATT PRUNTY's *Unarmed and Dangerous: New and Selected Poems* appeared in 1999. Six other collections of his poetry are available. His poems and essays have appeared in such periodicals as the *New Yorker,* the *New Republic, American Scholar, Parnassus, Boulevard,* and the *Yale Review.* Prunty serves as Carlton Professor of English at Sewanee where he edits the Sewanee Writers' Series and founded and directs the Sewanee Writers' Conference.

LEROY V. QUINTANA was born in New Mexico and served in the Long Range Reconnaissance Patrol/Airborne in Vietnam from 1967–1968. He has two daughters, Sandra, who is working on an M.A. in English at St. John's University in New York, and Elisa, who received a masters in physics and a masters in aerospace engineering from Michigan and is currently working on a Ph.D. Jose, thirteen, is working hard at skateboarding and playing the guitar. His wife, Yolanda, is a registered nurse. Quintana is the author of seven books of poetry and has been the recipient of an NEA grant.

BIN RAMKE edits the Contemporary Poetry Series for the University of Georgia Press and teaches at the University of Denver where he also edits the *Denver Quarterly*. He is the author of six books of poems, including *Massacre of the Innocents* and *Wake*. He was recently Distinguished Visiting Writer at the Art Institute of Chicago.

RON RASH has new poems in *Southern Review*, *Sewanee Review*, *Virginia Quarterly Review*, and *Prairie Schooner*. His first book of poems, *Eureka Mill*, was published in 1998 and his second poetry collection, *Among the Believers*, was published in 2000. He teaches at Tri-County Tech in Pendleton, South Carolina.

LIAM RECTOR's books of poems are *The Sorrow of Architecture* and *American Prodigal*. He edited *The Day I Was Older: On the Poetry of Donald Hall*. He is director of the graduate writing seminars at Bennington College and lives in the Boston area.

G. TRAVIS REGIER's work has appeared in *Poetry*, *Harper's*, *Atlantic Monthly*, *Quarterly West*, and *Ploughshares*, as well as several anthologies, including *The Winston Reader*, *Essays in Contemporary Culture*, and *An American Anthology*. He has been awarded a number of literary prizes, and two of his short stories have been made into independent films.

JACK RIDL has taught poetry writing at Hope College for twenty-nine years. He is the author of three collections of poems and coauthor with Peter Schakel of *Approaching Poetry: Perspectives and Responses*. The Carnegie Foundation named him Michigan's professor of the year. He lives with his wife, Julie, their two cats, and their two Clumber Spaniels.

LUIS J. RODRIGUEZ is the author of the best-selling memoir *Always Running: La Vida Loca: Gang Days in L.A.* His books of poetry are *Poems from the Pavement*, *The Concrete River*, and most recently *Trochemoche*. He received a Lannan Foundation Fellowship in 1992 and lives with his family in Chicago where he directs Tia Chucha Press.

PAUL RUFFIN's poems and stories have appeared in *Ploughshares*, *Southern Review*, *Poetry*, and *Georgia Review*. He has edited several anthologies, coedited scholarly books on John Steinbeck and William Goyen, and published four collections of poetry. He also writes a weekly column, "Ruffin-It," which appears in several newspapers in the South.

BENJAMIN ALIRE SAÉNZ is the author of two poetry books, *Calendar of Dust* and *Dark and Perfect Angels*, a collection of stories, *Flowers for the Broken*, two novels, *Carry Me Like Water* and *The House of Forgetting*, and two bilingual children's books, *A Gift for Papa Diego* and *Grandma Fina and Her Wonderful Umbrellas*. He is a former Wallace E. Stegner Fellow and in 1992 won an American Book Award. He works and lives and writes in El Paso, Texas, alongside his wife, Patricia Macias, who is an associate judge of the El Paso Children's Court. He has recently completed his third novel, *The Relics of Mourning*, and is working on a third book of poems, *Eschatologies*.

KATHERINE SÁNCHEZ is currently an M.F.A. student at the University of Florida. Her publishing credits include *Papyrus*, *Black Bear Review*, and *Oakland Review*.

SHEROD SANTOS is the author of three books of poetry and is a professor of English at the University of Missouri, Columbia. In 1998, Santos was awarded the B. F. Connors Long Poem Prize from the *Paris Review* for "Elegy for My Sister."

ARAM SAROYAN is the author of *O My Generation*, *Last Rites*, *Trio*, and most recently a novel, *The Romantic*. Twice the recipient of an NEA poetry award, Saroyan currently lives in California with his family.

HEATHER SELLERS is a native of Orlando, Florida. She taught for three years at the University of Texas, San Antonio, before moving to Michigan. She is currently an associate professor of English at Hope College. Her work appears in literary magazines such as *Field*, *Sun*, *Five Points*, and *Sonora Review*. She is currently at work on a novel, *Georgia Underwater*.

VIJAY SESHADRI was born in India and came to the United States in 1959 at the age of five. His poems, essays, and reviews have appeared in many magazines and anthologies, and he has received grants from the New York Foundation, Foundation for the Arts, and the NEA. His poetry collection, *Wild Kingdom*, was published in 1996. He currently lives in Brooklyn, New York, with his wife and son and works as a magazine editor, freelance writer, and teacher of poetry at Sarah Lawrence College.

VIVIAN SHIPLEY is editor of the *Connecticut Review* and is Distinguished Professor at Southern Connecticut State University. Raised in Kentucky, she has a Ph.D. from Vanderbilt University. She has won the Reader's Choice Award from *Prairie Schooner*, the Lucille Medwick Award from the Poetry Society of America, and the Ann Stanford Prize from the University of Southern California. *Devil's Lane*, published in 1996, was nominated for the Pulitzer

Prize. *How Many Stories?*, winner of *The Devil's Millhopper* chapbook contest, was published in 1998.

BARRY SILESKY's books include the biography of poet Lawrence Ferlinghetti, *Ferlinghetti: The Artist in His Time*; a collection of short-short fiction (or prose poems), *One Thing that Can Save Us*; a collection of verse, *The New Tenants*; and a prize-winning collection of prose poems, *In the Ruins*. His poems and fiction have appeared in magazines such as *Poetry, Boulevard, Witness, Grand Street, Poetry East, Fiction, Fiction International, Prose Poem*, and *Notre Dame Review*, and he writes literary reviews and articles for the *Chicago Tribune, American Book Review*, and other periodicals. He teaches writing and literature at the School of the Art Institute of Chicago.

R. T. SMITH was born in the District of Columbia and has lived in Georgia, North Carolina, Alabama, and Virginia. His family origins in the west of Ireland contribute to his interest in Irish literature and music, and he has received literature fellowships from the NEA, the Alabama Commission of the Arts, and Arts International. His most recent books are *Trespasser*, published in the U.S., and *Split the Lark: Selected Poems*, published in Ireland. Another collection, *Messenger* appeared in 2001. He currently edits *Shenandoah* and lives in Rockbridge County, Virginia.

DAVID STARKEY is associate professor of English at North Central College in Naperville, Illinois, and in 1999 was Fulbright Professor of English at the University of Oulu in Finland. Over the past twelve years, more than 250 of his poems have appeared in a number of anthologies and in literary journals in America, Britain, Canada, Australia, and New Zealand. In addition to publishing several collections of poems with small presses, he has written a textbook, *Poetry Writing: Theme and Variations*, and coedited, with Richard Guzman, an anthology of Chicago literature, *Smokestacks and Skyscrapers*.

MARK TAKSA's poems have appeared in *River City, Laurel Review*, and *Passages North*. *Cradlesong* won first prize in the 1993 National Looking Glass Poetry Chapbook Competition. His first poetry chapbook, *Truant Bather*, was published in 1986.

SUSAN THOMAS lives in northern Vermont where she writes, grows things, and, occasionally, teaches whatever she can. Her poems and short stories have appeared in many journals, most recently *Nimrod, Columbia, Confrontation, Feminist Studies*, and *New Delta Review*. Her collection of short stories was a finalist for the 1999 Bakeless Prize from Bread Loaf/Middlebury and she is a recipient of a 1999 Artist Development Grant from the Vermont Arts Council.

ANN TOWNSEND is the recipient of a "Discovery"/*The Nation* award, a grant from the Ohio Arts Council, and a fellowship from the Bread Loaf Conference. Her poems have appeared recently in *Five Points*, *TriQuarterly*, *Poetry*, *Southern Review*, and the *Nation*, and her first poetry collection, *Dime Store Erotics*, was published in 1998. She teaches creative writing at Denison University where she also directs the Jonathan Reynolds Young Writers Workshop.

WILLIAM TROWBRIDGE holds B.A. and M.A. degrees from the University of Missouri, Columbia, and a Ph.D. from Vanderbilt University. His books are *Flickers*, *O Paradise*, *Enter Dark Stranger*, and *The Book of Kong*. He is coeditor of the *Laurel Review*/Greentower Press.

SETH TUCKER, a native of Wyoming, is currently pursuing a Ph.D. in English at Florida State University. He received an M.A. from Northern Arizona University in 1998, where he served as poetry and fiction editor for *Thin Air*. Seth is a former Airborne Ranger who served in Panama and the Persian Gulf War. His most recent publications in fiction and poetry have appeared in *Mississippi Review*, *Spoon River Review*, and *Camphorweed*.

GLORIA VANDO's works have appeared in numerous literary magazines and anthologies, among them *Kenyon Review*, *Seattle Review*, *New Letters*, *Stiletto One*, *Rampike*, and *Kansas City Out Loud II*. She received the 1991 Billee Murray Denny Poetry Prize and was a finalist in the 1992 Walt Whitman Poetry Contest and the 1989 Poetry Society of America's Alice Fay DiCastagnola Award. She is the author of *Promesas: Geography of the Impossible*.

JUDITH VOLLMER's second full-length collection of poetry, *The Door Open to the Fire*, was awarded the Cleveland State University Poetry Center Prize. Vollmer, who directs the writing program at the University of Pittsburgh, Greensburg, also is the author of a chapbook, *Black Butterfly*, and *Level Green*. Vollmer coedits the poetry magazine *5 AM*.

MICHAEL WATERS is professor of English at Salisbury State University on the Eastern Shore of Maryland. His six books of poetry include *Green Ash, Red Maple, Black Gum*, *Bountiful*, *The Burden Lifters*, and *Anniversary of the Air*. His *New & Selected Poems* appeared in 2000, the same year his edition of *Contemporary American Poetry* was published. He has been the recipient of a fellowship in creative writing from the NEA, three Individual Artist Awards from the Maryland State Arts Council, and two Pushcart Prizes.

CHARLES HARPER WEBB is professor of English at California State University, Long Beach, as well as a psychotherapist in private practice. He has published a novel, *The Wilderness Effect*, and a book of poems, *Reading the Water*, and has edited two other collections of poetry. Mostly recently, he won the Felix Pollack Prize in poetry at the University of Wisconsin Press for his book *Liver*.

STEVE WILSON, whose books include *Allegory Dance* and *The Singapore Express*, was a recent Fulbright Scholar in creative writing in Transylvania. He has also taught and lived in Malaysia, Great Britain, and Ireland. His work has appeared in journals nationwide as well as in such recent anthologies as *What Have You Lost?* and *Best Texas Writing 2*. Wilson teaches at Southwest Texas State University.

MICHELE WOLF is the author of *Conversations During Sleep* and *The Keeper of Light*. Her poems have appeared widely in literary journals, including *Poetry*, *Hudson Review*, and *Boulevard*, and anthologies such as the award-winning *When I Am an Old Woman I Shall Wear Purple* and *I Am Becoming the Woman I've Wanted*. She has received an Anna Davidson Rosenberg Award for poems on the Jewish experience, been a National Arts Club Scholar in poetry at the Bread Loaf Writers' Conference, and been awarded residency fellowships by Yaddo, the Edward F. Albee Foundation, and the Virginia Center for the Creative Arts. Raised in Florida, she holds degrees from Boston University and Columbia. She lives in New York City where she works as a magazine writer and editor.

CAROLYNE WRIGHT has five books of poetry published, including *Premonitions of an Uneasy Guest* and *Seasons of Mangoes and Brainfire*, a collection of essays, *A Choice of Fidelities: Lectures and Readings from a Writer's Life*, and three volumes of poetry in translation from Spanish and Bengali. After other visiting creative writing posts at Emory University, the University of Wyoming, Sweet Briar College, Ashland University, and the University of Miami, she is visiting associate professor at Oklahoma State University, teaching poetry and creative nonfiction workshops in the M.A. and Ph.D. programs in creative writing.

PERMISSIONS

We are grateful to the authors who have given us permission to include previously unpublished work in this anthology. We also thank the authors, editors, and publishers who have given us permission to reprint poems.

Kim Addonizio, "Theodicy" and "From Then to Now," copyright © 1994 by Kim Addonizio. Reprinted from *The Philosopher's Club* by Kim Addonizio, with the permission of BOA Editions.

Liz Ahl, "Ammo," first published in *Slipstream*, appears by permission of the author.

Sandra Alcosser, "A Warrior's Tale," appears by permission of the author.

Sherman Alexie, "Texas Chainsaw Massacre," reprinted from *Old Shirts & New Skins* (University of California Press, 1993) by Sherman Alexie, appears by permission of the author.

William Baer, "Prosecutor," copyright © 1997 by William Baer. Reprinted from *The Unfortunates* by William Baer, first published by New Odyssey Press, appears by permission of the author.

David Baker, "Patriotics" and "More Rain," reprinted from *Sweet Home, Saturday Night* (University of Arkansas Press, 1991), appears by permission of the author.

Barry Ballard, "Hate Crime," first published in *Explorations 99* (University of Alaska), appears by permission of the author.

Jim Barnes, "For Roland, Presumed Taken," first published in *The Sawdust War* (University of Illinois Press, 1992), appears by permission of the author.

Edward Bartók-Baratta, "The Men Who Killed My Brother," appears by permission of the author.

Ellen Bass, "Bearing Witness," appears by permission of the author.

Jill Bialosky, "The Adolescent Suicide," appears by permission of the author.

Wendy Bishop, "Violence" and "Evidence of Death's Voodoo—Inside and Outside the 'Gun as Art Exhibit,'" first published in *Tonantzin*, appears by permission of the author.

Bruce Bond, "Aim," first published in *Radiography* (BOA Editions, 1997), appears by permission of the author.

John Bradley, "Improper Disposal," first published in *Aegean Review*, appears by permission of the author.

Sean Brendan-Brown, "The Dark Side of Dazzle," first published in *Indiana Review*, appears by permission of the author.

Gaylord Brewer, "Essays on Excess and Escape," appears by permission of the author.

Michael Bugeja, "Littleton" and "Shooter Rules," copyright © 1999 by Michael Bugeja. Reprinted from *Millennium's End* by Michael Bugeja, Archer Press, 1999, appears by permission of the author.

Brigitte Byrd, "Top Stories," appears by permission of the author.

Marcus Cafagña, "Lithium," first published in *Roman Fever* (Invisible Cities Press, 2001), appears by permission of the author.

TITLE INDEX

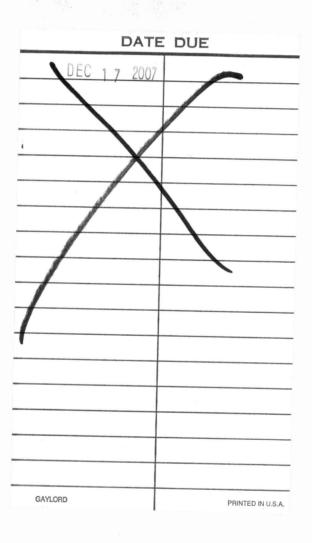

DATE DUE

DEC 17 2007